To our families—past, present, and future

**S.O. AND R.B.**

*"One can perfectly well philosophize while cooking supper."*

**SOR JUANA INEZ DE LA CRUZ**
**SELF-TAUGHT SCHOLAR, WRITER—MEXICO, 17TH CENTURY**

For information about this title or to order other books
and/or electronic media, contact the publisher:

Claws Out Press
clawsoutpress@gmail.com
www.anti-cookbook.com

ISBNs: 978-0-9975854-3-8 (softcover)
978-0-9975854-4-5 (eBook)

Printed in the United States of America
Cover and Interior design: 1106 Design
Illustrations: Olivia Bloom

# WHAT PEOPLE ARE SAYING

Shelley and Rebecca share their wisdom for living fully and that includes fantastic food ideas! *The Anti-Cookbook* not only offers any young person starting out on their own a foundation for living well in today's hurried world, but also strips away the often confining and intimidating process of eating well. The authors share their heart-filled stories and provide readers with valuable and important information about how to care for the world by respectfully choosing how and what we eat.

**YVONNE TALLY**
AUTHOR OF *BREAKING UP WITH BUSY, REAL-LIFE SOLUTIONS FOR OVERSCHEDULED WOMEN* AND CO-FOUNDER OF POISED INC.

*The Anti-Cookbook* is for the cook who needs a gentle nudge to start thinking out of the box when it comes to creating meals. Shelley and Rebecca not only give us delicious recipes, but they also show us that it's the journey that's inspiring the dishes. The duo are moms who understand the challenges of trying to get the kids to eat healthfully, with the eventual goal that they'll be cooking for themselves (cooking, that is, food that doesn't have the word "ramen" in it), as well as working women who know the value of time and money. If you are interested in the complexity of food choices, then you've picked up the right book.

**ALEX OTA**
CO-FOUNDER OF BREEZYMAMA.COM

In my first year fending for myself in the real world, learning how to procure quality meals while not breaking the bank has been a process. We're surrounded by an abundance of nutrition plans and food philosophies and it often seems more convenient to just eat out or order food for delivery. With entertaining personal commentary, *The Anti-Cookbook* boils it down to simple, timeless recipes that make learning how to prepare real home-cooked food feasible for any busy young professional trying to eat well for a reasonable price.

**OLIVIA NICHOLLS**
TECHNOLOGY MARKETING ASSOCIATE

# THE ANTI-COOKBOOK:

## *Easy, Thrifty Recipes for Food-Smart Living*

**By Shelley Onderdonk
and Rebecca Bloom**

# TABLE OF CONTENTS

# PREFACE

*The Anti-Cookbook: Easy, Thrifty Recipes for Food-Smart Living*, is a genre-bender. Why the title? Obviously we aren't against cooking! Instead, we are inverting the idea that cooking is simply about following a recipe. A "cookbook" method of completing a task implies a mundane, thoughtless process. This book seeks to do the opposite—to inspire readers to think creatively about making meals and independently about the deeper issues surrounding food and nourishment. One of our inspirations was *The Anti-Coloring Book,* which provided our children with hours of creative thinking; its guided projects promoted imagination over following rules. We attempt to do the same here for cooking. We're hoping to provide readers with a template for thoughtfulness around the way we feed ourselves. It's much more than measurements, heat, and chemistry, and that's what we unfold in these pages.

We are two mothers with a collection of recipes meant to be wholesome and a belief that cooking for yourself can be empowering in many ways. We believe that your food choices can affect your health, your pocketbook, and your mental state. Our hope is that our recipes and our stories about feeding our families and being fed by our forebears will resonate with you and bring more efficiency and joy to your food journey. We can't avoid the fact that we are two women who have spent an inordinate amount of time raising children, cooked for families nuclear and extended, and done it while maintaining our careers. So we have a slant, yes. But we also have some surprising contrasts in our experiences, which elucidate some larger truths about food and family.

Anyone can eat well with a lot of time and money. This book is for all of those who want to do so even if they have neither of those. It is inclusive of gender, age, race, and ethnicity, because everyone eats. It is especially for those who, for whatever reason (whether you are newly independent, have a young family, or are traveling), are a little overwhelmed by the prospect of preparing food. It can serve as an inspiration for those times when you are bereft of ideas. And above all, it is for everyone who is interested in the complex ethics of what we put in our mouths.

This book is for parents, their young-adult children, on-the-go people, and lifestyle "hackers" far and wide who are sick of the word "hack" being used in every sentence. You don't *hack* your life—you *hack* an organic potato and cook it till the edges are crispy.

It's for idealists and realists, environmentalists, and simplifiers. And for anyone who is looking for healthful, economical, and reasonable strategies for eating well and being a respectful human being on planet Earth—without all the stress and added sodium.

Some readers are going to revel in the stories. Others will skip right to the recipes and listicles. It's a book to enjoy and to refer back to—like my husband's recipe for tuna steaks with *cipollini*—simple and nourishing. The hope is that you'll use it to make memories as well as meals.

## Tuna Steaks With Cipollini
### PREP TIME: 45 MINUTES

*Peel 1 lb. of cipollini onions; place in a large baking pan. Make a mixture of ¼ cup of olive oil and ½ cup of balsamic vinegar. Whisk in salt and pepper. Coat the onions, and then pour the rest evenly throughout the pan. Meanwhile, marinate approximately 1 lb. of tuna steaks in ¼ cup of olive oil and the juice of 2 lemons. Roast the onions for about 40 minutes at 350 degrees. Cook the tuna in a separate pan for about 15-20 minutes. Serve with onions on top of the tuna, rice, and/or a green salad.*

# INTRODUCTION

It's hot in New York City. I'm walking down the street with my firstborn, lugging stuff from Bed Bath & Beyond. The verboten plastic bag handles are cutting into my fore-arms. My phone buzzes in my pocket. My hands are too full to arrange looking at it, but I expect it is something from my younger daughter, already starting her senior year across the country—California still hasn't gotten the Labor Day memo. I imagine a sad-lipped Snapchat of her wilting in a classroom with no air-conditioning with a "Dying..." caption.

I'm here to settle my older daughter in. She's decided to take the plunge and move to New York after college graduation. Job is still up in the air, but, lucky for her, she can start out living with my parents. The price is right. But she wants to earn her keep, so the thought is to get her up and running with the right small appliances and kitchen tools so she can cook for herself and her grandparents—they eat out a lot, and this would be good for everyone. It's a bold experiment!

When I arrive at the apartment, I put down the packages and have a seat on the couch that will double as my daughter's bed for the months to come. I check my phone. Nothing from the "little one", as I like to call her, though she has at least four inches on me. But there's a delightful e-mail from one of my college roommates. We recently worked on a book together that she co-wrote with her husband, and we've had some amazing visits in the last few years. Shelley has an idea. Since she's one of my favorite writers, excerpts are the right editorial decision:

*Hi Rebecca!*

*I hope you and family are well. I am contacting you because I have an idea for a book, and I think you may be my perfect coauthor if you are interested and have the time. This is my idea: you and I are both in the throes of children moving out, and I have recently found myself working, at his behest, to equip Dylan (both literally and figuratively) to live on his own in his first apartment. My thoughts have run from the essentials of cookware to guides on grocery shopping to recipes to cooking lessons. And as I have started to com-pile all this, I realized that "cooking your way to independence" is a theme that is quite near and dear to my heart. From varied perspectives—an environmental stand against fast food, health, budget—there are many reasons to embrace learning to cook. I won't bore you with any more details, but lmk if you are interested in it...Just another crazy Saturday in my mind.*

*Xoxoxo*

*S*

Crazy? Nope, more like kismet. Though we've lived very different lives since college—Shelley on the East Coast, a veterinarian, raising boys and horses, me a transplanted New York lawyer raising girls in Silicon Valley (where Shelley grew up) and now working as a writer and editor—we have what I like to call a "common core" (with apologies to all those who suffer because of that top-down, micro-management, education disaster), some notably similar values and habits. Among what we share is a holistic concern about food: how it is grown, harvested, distributed, prepared, and consumed. We are both earnest and purposeful people. Okay, I'm snarkier—but I come by it honestly.

When I think deeply about this, I realize this project is no accident. Shelley and I started "adulting" in a college apartment our senior year. We shopped, cooked, cleaned, and communed on a budget—I'd like to think, with some flair. For sure, our apartment kitchen was more inviting and better used than the jocks' across the hall—they had towers of pizza boxes in the foyer. We brought together what we knew from our parents and grandparents and experimented with foods that neither of us knew anything about. We mixed it all up and made it work. And we hardly ever ordered in. We didn't have the money, but we also found joy in taking care of ourselves and each other.

It turns out that our lives, though far-flung after college, have converged meaningfully. This is beautifully exemplified by the parallel situations of our two eldest kids. Post-college, they both find themselves trying to make life work in New York City. My original home turf. The world just keeps on turning.

You might ask why two competent people who set about designing their lives and families with such care found themselves with two kids in their early twenties who want or need this kind of life-coaching. Well, that's a book unto itself, but thank goodness it has already been written. There's been a cultural shift during the generation in which we raised our kids. When we started, it was all about attachment parenting. It was a contact sport. We trained for it, and we were emotionally open. But, somewhere around the time that our eldest kids became teens, something changed. All of a sudden, the "helicopter" metaphor dominated the national conversation, and we were supposed to back off and quit hovering. Both rule followers, we tried. But our oldest children were already ensconced in their over-committed, stressful lives, careening toward the goal of coveted college acceptances. It wasn't so simple to pull back. Shelley drove hours to soccer practices while I ran around between art and dance lessons and babysat hours of marathon homework stints. We both probably tried to do everything we could to teach our kids about healthy, wholesome living habits, but there wasn't much time for them to be hands-on. And then they went to college. There, they continued striving and mincing words, but not fresh garlic.

As our children take their leave, embarking upon their adult lives, we're both trying to pass on some essential values as we give them cooking crash courses, often via text-message. We want them to see it as an expression of family, tradition, and mindfulness. As a species, our relationship with the earth has become ever tenuous, and we both want our progeny to go out into the world with the tools they need to tread respectfully. Not to mention that they'll go broke if they don't reckon with the fact that they can flip their own damn omelet.

## Basic Omelet

PREP TIME: 5 MINUTES

*Whisk 3 eggs. Pour into pan over low heat—you may be tempted to turn up the heat to speed things up. Don't do it! Add cheeses and veggies of your choice. Fold into thirds, and cook until egg is solid. Flip, if needed.*

# HOW FOOD DEFINES US

*You can tell a lot about people by what's in their cupboards*

Do you look into other people's grocery carts in the checkout line? Peer into restaurants to see what people are eating? Most of us have an innate curiosity about what we, as a species, consume, whether it be a choice between a chai and a café latte or veal scaloppine and pasta al pesto. And that is because what we eat characterizes us in so many ways. There are cultural, historic, convenience, and moral reasons behind what we pick up with our forks, chopsticks, or fingers. We are no exception—our pasts have shaped our culinary interests.

By way of introduction, I'd say that I, Rebecca Bloom, am someone who fights hard to self-define. I rage against every stereotype, and that is my essence, so to list me as the grandchild of Ashkenazi Jewish immigrants who came to New York and the child of suburban strivers living their American dream is probably not going to get you all the way there. I'm a person of contrasts—glib yet sincere, serious and funny, mature but in touch with youthful energy. I'm a fighter and a lover. I have never believed that complex individuals have to embody one side or the other of what we think of as correlative opposites. Starting with me.

Hailing from New York, I wouldn't say that I turn to one easily identifiable style of food as a base. There's no such thing as "New York" food—the whole pizza-and-bagel vortex is overblown. There are so many ethnicities and endless specialties in that teeming city. I have tried, with mixed results, to love the cuisine of my people—largely Eastern European Jews. *Babka* was easy, and the same for *rugelach*, but things like *gefilte fish* always grossed me out. Thank goodness for the magic of *matzah brei*; it is truly delicious and not unhealthy. It packs all the good memories of my grandparents. My grandfather was a butter-and-egg man (as well as a public school teacher and summer-camp owner) and the best jelly-omelet maker in the Catskill Mountains. He made us *matzah brei* at Passover, and this easy recipe is one for the books.

### Matzah Brei

PREP TIME: 15 MINUTES

*Wet a few pieces of matzah in a bowl. When it is softened, break it into small pieces, about an inch in diameter. Cook half a shallot or a quarter of a chopped onion in butter or olive oil. Coat the pan fully, and pour in 6-8 scrambled eggs. Add the matzah, and cook the eggs as you normally would. Salt and pepper to taste. You can add spinach for some green or just prepare a side salad.*

After college, I lived in Italy and learned to cook by imitating those around me. That's when I fell in love with vegetables and grains—it was what I could afford, and there were so many things I'd never seen before. I learned about artichokes, blood oranges, *farro,* and the bounty of nature. I went to the central market in Florence and saw "what was good today" and reacted accordingly. I felt like an alchemist, blending flavors, discovering classic combinations, and thinking about ways to riff on them. To me, cooking and eating a mostly plant-based diet became like the endless loop of a jazz combination—with permutations that would be good as long as the fundamentals were sound.

The first time I ever saw tuna and beans together was in Italy. Great flavors, easy to make. Non-dairy. Cheap! Looks like you tried and you know what you're doing.

## Salad with Tuna, White Beans, and Shallots
### PREP TIME: 15 MINUTES

*Drain the tuna. Slice some shallots thinly (maybe half of a regular-sized one), and cook them in some olive oil at low heat for about two minutes. Sauté the drained beans in with the shallots for about another two minutes, and put the tuna in the pan at the last minute, just for a stir or two. Add some lemon juice or red wine vinegar for a splash of flavor, add a few turns of the pepper mill, and you're done. Can be eaten with a fork over some salad greens or as a bruschetta mixture on some sliced rustic bread.*

*Variations: Vegan with tofu: Add red grapes for some color and sweetness!*

I remember making rice, sautéing vegetables, and trying things out with Shelley in our college kitchen. We were all on a budget, and we did our best. We didn't even have a table. We probably had one pan, one pot, one spatula, a few knives, and a cutting board.

I, Shelley Onderdonk, remember that, in our first apartment, senior year of college, the refrigerator was divided by shelf, but we always shared eating carrots dipped in mustard out of the fridge. We lived on Pong Pong sauce—a peanut butter-based Asian sauce that was delicious on noodles or rice.

**Pong Pong Sauce**

PREP TIME: 5 MINUTES

*Anytime you have about ¼ jar of peanut butter left, make Pong Pong sauce in the jar. Just add about 3 tbsp. each of sesame oil, tamari, and rice wine vinegar until the consistency is just about pourable. Then add chopped scallions, garlic, and ginger. Stores in the fridge longer than you will need it to, as it is yummy on any carb you can think of. I particularly like it on soba noodles.*

**Pong Pong sauce was one of the first recipes my son asked for when he moved out:**

What's the recipe for ur Asian peanut sauce thing

There were many firsts in that apartment—daily reading of the *New York Times* and learning from an Indian friend how to make *dal*—are two of the more mentionable ones.

## Dal

**PREP TIME: 1 HOUR AND 15 MINUTES**

*Sauté 2 cups yellow or orange lentils, 1 potato, 2 carrots, onions, garlic, and ginger with olive oil and salt and curry powder in a large pot until onions are soft. Fill the pot about halfway up with boiling water. Cook 1 hour. Add any other vegetables later, such as broccoli or zucchini squash.*

Rebecca and I were from different coasts—NY and CA—but shared a predilection for early-morning runs and healthy eating. Certainly a primary motivator of living off campus was to be able to cook for myself—vegetarian options in the dining hall had pretty much confined me to the salad bar for three years—and I found a perfect partner in Rebecca, who always embodied to me the essence of NYC cool, but somehow didn't mind living with me.

Starting out to write this book together, almost thirty years later, we initially explored who we were in the context of our project. I discovered some remarkable things in the search. I did find what I was looking for—my folder from veterinary school when I headed up our chapter of an animal-welfare organization. It had the information about living conditions of what was referred to in school as a "food animal" which, itself, was somewhat oxymoronic for a veterinary student interested in the value of an animal's life. I found my long-lost senior thesis, which honestly was a little boring to read (if I give myself the benefit of the doubt, it is maybe because what I wrote about was so prescient that, in 2018, it is mundane). I dug up love letters and incriminating photos. And obviously, I discovered my heretofore-unknown proclivity to procrastinate, as I succeeded in filling six bags with books to take to Goodwill, alphabetizing my entire library, and organizing decades worth of random clippings from the days before the Internet, before I succeeded in writing a single word on the topic I was supposed to pursue.

I am from the San Francisco Bay area, and my husband accuses me of being able to eat Mexican 3 times a day. I say, "Why not?" California used to be part of Mexico, anyway. And it is a fabulous cuisine to do pescatarian. I personally will prepare Mexican, though, only if I have at least one good avocado. If I have it, game on.

## Tacos

**PREP TIME: 30 MINUTES**

*"Make your own tacos" is a great way to please a variety of guests, as everyone can choose their own fillings. And the leftovers can feed you for days for breakfast, lunch, or dinner. Buy tortillas, and offer some or all of the following: rice, beans (see p. 18), fish, tofu (see p. 7), tomato salsa, mango salsa, guacamole (recipe on p. 85), shredded cheese, grilled veggies such as onions, mushrooms, peppers and/or zucchini (recipe on p. 87), sour cream, and hot sauce.*

When I was teaching in Hong Kong after college graduation, my parents came for a visit. Their first evening, I took them to experience what was to me a quintessentially Chinese ritual—shopping for dinner at the local outdoor market stalls. Faced with wire cages of chickens and ducks, and buckets of fish and eels, my carnivorous father decided to eat vegetarian with me for dinner. Making a decision on which greens to buy seemed infinitely easier than deciding which eyes you could consign to oblivion! I perfected my stir-fry in a tiny kitchen in an apartment in Kowloon Tong—the same cramped room in which I experienced a gecko crawling up my leg. I've never moved so fast as when I saw that tail disappearing up my pant cuff. . . .

## Stir-Fried Vegetables

**PREP TIME: 20 MINUTES**

*I learned to stir fry in Hong Kong, using a combination of water, sesame oil, and soy sauce in a wok. Now I use tamari and walnut oil in a cast-iron pan. Times change; adults become pickier. But the principle remains the same: start with ginger, garlic, and onion, add harder vegetables (e.g., carrots) first and then mushrooms to bring out their flavor. Then add in zucchini and/or broccoli. Add water as you go along if you need to add more steam power. Everything should get soft at the same time. Use the same pan to fry tofu cubes in sesame oil and soy sauce, turning once. Serve together over rice, and it's a meal. Make sure the rice is ready, because this cooks quickly!*

*Tofu cooking tip: when you start the rice, also pop the tofu cubes in a 200-degree oven on a greased baking sheet. They will dehydrate a bit, and, when it is time to stir-fry them, it will be much easier to attain crispy edges.*

My husband and I spent one lovely August in an old farmhouse on the outskirts of Deauville, France, that had vegetable beds. The owners ran a bed-and-breakfast, and their parting words before they took off for their vacation were, "Help yourself to the garden." That summer I learned to cook what was available—what a pleasure it was to go outside and pick something, and then figure out how to cook or prepare it. Planning ahead with lists and trips to the grocery store was replaced by an atavistically satisfying method of eating what you gathered. If you ever have cucumbers and dill in the garden, try eating this:

## Cucumber Salad

PREP TIME: 10 MINUTES

*Peel, seed, and slice cucumbers. Add salt, pepper, fresh dill, crème fraiche, and Dijon mustard and lemon juice to taste.*

That summer I also learned from the wise French innkeeper how helpful it was to have the cooking oils in a cabinet abutting the range, for easy reach. That is a mundane tip but a nugget of wisdom equally as valuable as the more sublime lessons I have spent a lot of my life thinking about—how food intersects with health, environmental steward-ship, and animal welfare. I hope in these pages to help people understand how these multiple-times-a-day choices have profound consequences.

It has also occurred to me that I have some skin in the game—I am perhaps writing this book to gain a sense of closure. About twenty-three years ago, my life was upended (for the better, I might add) with the birth of my first son, and, ever since, I have attempted to be the woman who can do it all. But that responsibility is exhausting. At age fifty, I feel a little like I have been on a long detour; a mother starts to find a sense of self again once the youngest child is older. To celebrate that commencement, what better way than to pass on the baton of cooking?

# CHAPTER II

# COOKING YOUR WAY TO INDEPENDENCE

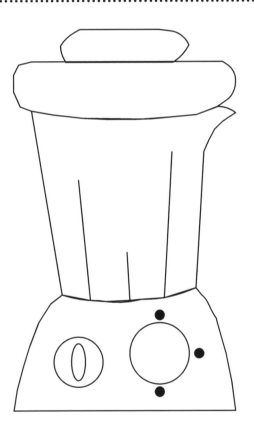

*We want readers to see the sweetness of committing to themselves, to locally sourced ingredients and wholesome recipes, to sitting down to a homemade meal instead of dialing one up or paying someone else to cut the broccoli*

Self-sufficiency in the kitchen is a big hurdle to achieving adulthood. And as my oldest child is setting off and moving toward independence after graduating from college, one of my worst nightmares is that my child will resort to buying a chunk of meat every night because it is the easiest thing to cook! Or he will become that person who doesn't cook and severely compromises his health by eating too many processed foods or compromises his ethics by supporting fast-food conglomerates.

I remember having a conversation with Rebecca freshman year in which we got pretty philosophical, for eighteen-year-olds, about parents and kids. She wondered aloud if parents of our generation actually understood who their kids were. I just sort of shrugged my shoulders and said that it was natural, that kids are supposed to evolve beyond their parents. I think she looked at me a little wide-eyed, but she sort of got my weird mixture of hubris melded with biological thinking. However, now I feel it from the other end—that I want my children to succeed beyond my small successes; giving the next generation a boost so that they don't have to tread the same ground I have already covered is part of the reason for my writing this book. What follows is a distillation of the most basic and straightforward information to getting started cooking, beginning with helpful advice for setting up a kitchen.

## KITCHEN BASICS

### GO-TO SPICE CABINET

Sea salt grinder

Pepper grinder

Oregano

Basil

Cinnamon

Nutmeg

Allspice

Turmeric

Paprika

Cayenne Pepper

Chili Powder

Garlic Powder

Sesame Seeds

Thyme

Celery seeds

### TOOLS YOU NEED

Knives

Spatula

Wooden spoons

Vegetable peeler

Rubber spatula

Whisk

Baking sheet

Pasta pot

Colander

2 sizes cast-iron frying pans

Soup/oatmeal pot

Hot mitts

### SMALL APPLIANCES YOU NEED

Panini grill

Blender

Rice Cooker

### SMALL APPLIANCES YOU PROBABLY WANT

Hand mixer

Electric teakettle

French press

Coffee grinder

Citrus juicer

Toaster

### SMALL APPLIANCES NOT TO WASTE YOUR MONEY ON

Bread maker

Fancy food chopper

Electric mixer

Juicer

Fancy coffee maker

## The return on a small investment:

Chef extraordinaire w new smoothie maker!

A smoothie is a classic snack or on-the-go meal with endless variations. Understand the basics, and experiment from there. It is the universally first item my boys learned to make themselves. Score.

## Standard Smoothie

PREP TIME: 5 MINUTES

1 serving

**Place in blender:**

- ❏ ½ banana, fresh or frozen*
- ❏ 1 cup fruit, fresh or frozen
- ❏ ½ cup almond milk
- ❏ ½ cup yogurt
- ❏ ½ cup juice**
- ❏ handful walnuts
- ❏ 1 tbsp. ground flax and/or chia seeds***

\* *peel and freeze old-ish bananas to use in smoothies*

\*\* *organic apple juice or POM are my favorites with berries as fruit, but orange can be good in some smoothies, such as with peaches for fruit*

\*\*\* *keeping a mixture of these ground in the fridge is a great way to have these nutritional powerhouses on hand. You can use a coffee grinder to grind them. Seeds in the teeth are no fun!*

***Nutritional boost:*** *add a few leaves of baby kale*

I initially got our family eating quesadillas on the trail. They are a warm, morale-boosting treat in the wilderness but equally satisfying at home. Great for independent cooking, they are the second thing my boys learned how to make on their own. Independence tip: backpacking in the wilderness is a natural teacher of food self-sufficiency.

## Quesadilla

**PREP TIME: 5 MINUTES**

*Heat up a panini grill. In a large tortilla, add your choice of the following: grated cheese, tomatoes, spinach or arugula, avocado, salsa, turkey, or ham slices. Cook for about 3-4 minutes.*

**Spice tip:** *add fresh jalapeno*
**Time-saving tip:** *assemble quesadilla on a large plate you can also use for eating*
**Kitchen appliances:** *Panini grill or large non-stick skillet.*

For another easy-as-pie recipe (whoever thought up that idiom is crazy—I don't think pies are easy!), try this one on. I made repeated attempts at home to copy a delicious crispy *gnocchi* we would get from the local pizza joint, which was a completely different take on starchy *gnocchi*. But it never worked. It was always sticky. One day, my daughter ended up finding a hint online—it suggested we lose the boiling water. That was a revelation.

## Easy Pan-Toasted Gnocchi

**PREP TIME: 15 MINUTES**

*Saute half of a minced shallot and ½ tsp. minced garlic in 1 tbsp. olive oil in a skillet on low heat until translucent, but not browned. Turn the heat up to medium, and add fresh gnocchi. Quick-stir until golden-brown. What could be easier? Serve with sauce and veggie of choice. Or don't!*

**This text arrived out of the blue one evening:**

**Tried and True**

**Impressive!!**

**always the tone of surprise - ron**

I love to see the evidence that my child cooked and ate a healthy meal (in this case, it's stir-fried vegetables); it's more satisfying than eating one myself. But I must admit two things on this one: I am guilty as charged—I am still *pleasantly* surprised by kitchen successes; and it took me a few readings to get the *Harry Potter* reference.

Ever notice how often people turn to soup for comfort and nutrition? Think about how you see it on restaurant menus and in advertisements for prepared products. They usually describe it in nostalgic terms like "Grandma's Classic Tomato Soup." They know what they're doing—and they know what you want. Part of cooking your way to independence is mastering basic vegetable purees yourself. Don't let the food-industrial complex fool you with fancy garnishes and words like "hearty" or "bisque" or "creamy"—you've got this! With a modest quantity of zucchini, broccoli, cauliflower, carrots, or butternut squash, you can make amazing vegetable purees at home at a fraction of the cost with just a stockpot and a blender inside of an hour. And you can jazz it up with garnishes, toppings, and fun toast or breadsticks easily as well. So, what does this look like? Here's a template to work with:

## Zucchini Soup

- ❏ 2 tbsp. of olive oil
- ❏ 1 small red onion (or half a large one)
- ❏ 4 cloves of garlic
- ❏ 4 large or 8 small zucchini, cut and quartered
- ❏ 2 cups of vegetable broth
- ❏ 2 cups of coconut milk (optional, but optimal if you like your soup creamy)
- ❏ Juice of 2 lemons
- ❏ Salt and pepper to taste

*Saute onions and garlic in olive oil at low heat until translucent. Add zucchini, and continue to cook until they "sweat" and turn bright green, about 10-15 minutes. Add broth, coconut milk, and lemon juice, and simmer another 5 minutes. Pour into a blender (in 1 batch or 2), and blend to desired consistency. Put it back on the stove, and simmer another 10-15 minutes. Serve with salted rustic toast or breadsticks. Garnish with seeds, red pepper flakes, roasted nuts, fresh parsley, lemon slices, or whatever you think will look and taste right.*

**Shelley's tip:** If you like making soups, buy an immersion blender. They are cheap, tidy to store, and will prevent you from cleaning up soup particles from walls and ceilings when you inevitably overfill your blender with hot liquid and watch the top fly off.

For broccoli or cauliflower, keep the lemon if you like it, and use a "head" of either. For carrots, stick with about the same quantity as the zucchini, but lose the lemon and consider an extra flavor like curry or cumin. For butternut squash, add some cooking time, maybe an extra ten minutes. Other garnishes could include a dollop of Greek yogurt, some smaller pieces of baguette toast (with or without a bit of melted cheese) to serve in the soup as opposed to on the side, or some freshly sliced apples or pears topped with some balsamic vinegar.

# CHAPTER III

# SAVE TIME, SAVE MONEY

*Tips and tricks you can use*

An old adage about New York City: you can't possibly have a great apartment, a great partner, and a great job at the same time. Like most truisms, this may not prove entirely true, but it is laced with some useful realism. To find the balance you seek, you have to prioritize. When it comes to time and money, there's a corollary—you're either long on one or the other, but you generally do not have both (and many hard-working people feel they have neither). We'd like to save you time and money.

## Tips for Stretching Your Food Budget

1. Buy dry: beans and lentils. In general, dried beans can be soaked overnight and then drained and rinsed the following day before cooking.

### Black-Eyed Pea Stew

PREP TIME: 30 MINUTES

A cheap and lovely variation on a southern classic.

*Cook the peas according to directions. While they are cooking, sauté onion, garlic, carrots, and celery with oil and salt. When peas are soft, add veggies, fresh thyme, and spinach. Serve with tortillas or rice or corn bread.*

> **Rebecca's take:** It's true, the dried beans and lentils are cheaper. And, really, it isn't such a big deal to pressure-cook them, soak them, or cook them properly another way. And I'd feel better about myself if I did this. But, honestly, I don't. I've had too many meals where the beans are still crunchy, and I feel virtuous enough eating beans and lentils as it is.

2. Buy frozen: fish and fruit especially, not only because they are cheaper but also because they are often better quality and won't go to waste.

3. Think simple: a tomato, cut up and sautéed in olive oil with a little garlic and salt, makes a delicious and cheap pasta sauce.

4. Grow your own: on most windowsills, you can grow a few herbs. Thyme, mint, parsley, oregano, and basil are all resilient. With a bit more space, try growing greens such as arugula or kale. They are virtually indestructible, and you can pick a few leaves for a free nutritional boost at any time.

5. Reduce, reuse, recycle: keep old glass containers (such as peanut-butter jars and jelly jars) for free, BPA-free leftover food-storage containers.

6. Buy generic: some grocery stores have successfully based their entire business model upon this maxim (Trader Joe's, for example), but even at Whole Foods, Kroger, or other large chains, generic is the way to go for affordability.

## Meals in Less Than Ten Minutes

You know that moment when it is already eight in the evening and you just wrapped up work? You need to eat, shower, stretch, and reclaim some personal time. It would be so easy to order in right now. What can you do instead?

1. I'll opt for opening a can of soup and eating it with toast or crackers every time. Look for BPA-free cans, and buy organic soups in bulk when they go on sale. Always a necessity to have in my cupboard.

2. Frozen pizzas are also an excellent standby. To spice up a plain cheese pie, crack a raw egg in the middle, cook on a rack high in the oven, and/or place arugula or spinach on top.

3. Reheat anything you have in the fridge in a frying pan, and crack an egg or two on top; serve with toast. Almost always works!

4. See Smoothie and Quesadilla recipes from previous chapter.

## One-Pot Meals

I always make soups and stews in one pot. I just sauté whatever is going in the dish in the big soup pot with olive oil. Then I add water that I've already boiled in my electric tea-kettle. Lazy-woman's way, but I really don't notice any difference. I am all about reducing cleanup time!

## A Trio Template

Successful independent living is a lot about time management and thus goes hand-in-hand with efficiency. And, for efficiency's sake, there is nothing like spending three hours cooking. A rainy Sunday morning, a canceled appointment, or a day too hot or cold or windy to enjoy being outside are all good excuses. You start by brewing a soup or stew, so it can simmer during the rest of the process. Next, preheat the oven for a baking project, and, finally, assemble some kind of a salad that can be refrigerated. A trio like this can form the basis of a week's worth of healthy eating. Just add to the shopping list a loaf of bread or pita, fruit, and eggs, hummus, or other animal protein, and you are set.

### Curried Lentil Soup

PREP TIME: 20 MINUTES—FASTER, IF YOU CHOP QUICKLY

*Sauté 1 onion, 1 bulb garlic, a couple of carrots and celery stalks, and 1 sweet potato in a large soup pot with olive oil. Add curry powder (about 2 tbsp. to start), salt, about 1 cup lentils, and ¼ cup brown rice. Sauté until onions are soft. Add hot water (ideally boiled from teapot, about 2 liters); then turn down to simmer for 1 hour.*

### Granola

PREP TIME: 15 MINUTES

This has been my most-asked-for recipe, so much so that I have it on "notes" on my phone so I can forward it easily. Isn't everyone looking for a great way to start the day?

*Toast 1-2 cups of assorted raw chopped nuts (almonds, pecans, walnuts, hazelnuts) on a large cookie sheet for 10 minutes at 300 degrees. When done, empty into large glass container and let cool. Turn oven to 350 degrees.*

**Meanwhile, mix in medium bowl:**

- ❏ 6 cups organic rolled oats
- ❏ 1 cup assorted raw seeds (sunflower, pumpkin, ground flax)
- ❏ Pinch salt
- ❏ ⅓ cup oil (flax or canola)
- ❏ ⅓ cup maple syrup

*Spread oat mix on cookie sheet, and bake for 25-30 minutes at 350 degrees. Let cool in pan. Add oat mixture to nuts, and add about 1 cup dried fruit. Store in airtight container.*

## Bean, Barley, and Greens Salad

### PREP TIME: 30 MINUTES

*Cook 1 cup barley in 3 cups water until tender. Drain. Add 2 cups baby greens (swiss chard, spinach, or kale), 1 chopped or grated carrot, and about ½ cup scallions, shallots, or onion to the pot, and cover to let steam.*

*Eventually add 1 can beans (garbanzo, black or white Italian), 1 cup feta cheese, and dressing of olive oil and fresh lemon juice and lemon zest and salt. Use fresh parsley, mint, and oregano, if you have them, about 1 cup total chopped, or 1 tsp. each dried.*

Another idea for a trio you can find in these pages: Split-pea soup (p. 86), muffins (p. 69), and Mediterranean salad (p. 36).

## A Note About Timing

When you start putting together a meal, it can be hard to know what to do first. Obviously, you'll start by boiling the water and cooking onions or garlic in oil until they are translucent. But how do you know how to time other stuff? Start from the top—whatever takes the longest, you do first. If you're cooking vegetables, you start with what's thickest and most dense, and taper down. Usually meat, fish, chicken, or tofu starts before the sides, but rice takes longer than couscous, pasta, or quinoa. A helpful hint is to literally list things in a quick timeline. It could look something like this:

Baked potatoes or rice—45 minutes

Tuna—20 minutes

Sautéed spinach—5 minutes

Set the oven timer (or your phone) at 45 minutes when you start the potatoes. Pop the tuna in the oven when it hits 20. Cook up the spinach when the clock counts down to 5.

## Finding the Right Balance: to DIY or not to DIY

We know all about the best-laid plans, and we're not trying to preach. The fact is, you can make all your own sauces, pie crusts, and fresh pasta with the right tools, regular hours, and a super low-key social life (how's that for a euphemism?). If you did this, sure, you might save a few bucks. But we're not asking you to go monastic. The sometimes self-righteous glow of doing it yourself can be balanced against the convenience of some totally solid, ready-made shortcuts. How about some help assessing your options? There are so many, and we have it on good authority that the pros and cons are not always intuitive.

### BASIC TOMATO SAUCE:

To make your own, at a minimum, you need canned or fresh tomatoes, minced garlic, olive oil, tomato paste, oregano, salt, and pepper. There are many ways to get fancier, but that's the basic recipe. You can eat this after quick cooking, but if you don't simmer it for at least an hour or two, you will have a less-developed flavor profile. If you don't have the time or the ingredients and you want to make something with tomato sauce after work, many stores make sauce fresh and package it up. It won't be cheaper, but you can get it for a ready-to-go dinner in a small quantity. Some days, that works. On other days, splurge on a jar of a brand you like. You're still cooking at home, right?

### BROTH:

Be it vegetable, chicken, or beef, this basic can be tackled in a few ways. You can start with bullion and water, which is cheap and efficient. You can make your own, which is fun but time consuming, or you can buy some ready-made with low sodium and organic options available at most stores. But wait—there's more. You can boil down vegetables and spices into a paste and keep it in a jar in the fridge to use as a starter. I've always wanted to do that and I have seen it in friends' kitchens. The verdict? Do what works for you.

### PIZZA CRUST:

I'll just say it: making pizza dough is satisfying, but it is a mess. So many stores carry fresh or frozen pizza dough, and you can still have fun with toppings without having to mop up all the flour that's going to get all over your kitchen floor.

### GRATED CHEESE:

Get a hold of yourself: you do not need to pay for someone else to grate your cheese. It costs a fortune! When you do it yourself, it is fresher, and all you need is a simple cheese grater and two minutes.

As it turns out, everyone picks their poison. You will, too. For I, Shelley, choose the exact opposite of Rebecca—I almost always make my own pizza crust and buy grated cheese. I guess I think it is a lot easier to clean up floured counters than cheese graters!

### Pizza Dough

*Simply mix 1¼ cup warm water, 1 tbsp. dry yeast, ½ tbsp. sea salt, 1 tbsp olive oil, and 3 cups flour in large bowl. Knead on floured surface until dough is smooth and springy. Put back into bowl, cover, and let rise in a warm place.*

### RICED CAULIFLOWER:

See grated cheese, please.

### PRE-CUT VEGETABLES:

Nope. Why did you bother with knives and cutting boards? Wash it and cut it, and be done. Unless you're dealing with butternut squash or pumpkin, then we get it.

**FRESH PASTA:**

Right up there with pizza dough in the mess department, times two. If you're chilling on the weekend, and you want to do it the way *Nonna* did it, go for it. During the week, please just buy it! If it busts your budget, buy quality dry pasta, and shave a minute or two off the cooking time to get that delicious *al dente* thing happening.

**PRE-WASHED SALAD:**

No question, this does save you time and is especially convenient when you're cooking for one. It costs more and is probably a little bit less fresh, but enough years of dinners on the run has shown that there are worse things you could do.

**PIE CRUST:**

Not for the faint of heart. If you are a great baker, you can certainly try to make your own. But please don't hate on yourself if you pick one up at the store and fill it with fruit.

**SMOOTHIES/JUICES:**

Nobody is trying to ruin your fun. If going out for an $8-$12 green juice is your weekend's entertainment with a friend, that's a bizarre wrinkle of modern life, but no judgment. When you are at home in your own kitchen, however, all it takes is a blender and a dream.

**ARTISAN BREAD:**

If you love to do it, get after it. Practically speaking, you'd probably be best served baking bread on the weekends. If ever you find yourself at a loss for a great dinner plan, however, beautiful bread can make a meal and might be the splurge you need after a busy day.

# CHAPTER IV

# FISH AND COFFEE

*Making choices in an ethically complex world*

A few years ago, I settled upon the phrase "ethical eating" to best describe my attitude toward food. It summons to mind the complex stew of choices one confronts when buying and eating food. Coffee is a great example—is it more important to have fair-trade, shade-grown, or organic beans? This is the intersection of human labor, environmental responsibility, and consumer health that is a part of every trip to the grocery store, and that is when it is not even an animal product! I am not going to quibble with someone over whether they'd rather buy free-trade and preserve a farmer's livelihood in central America, or buy organic beans because they don't want pesticides in their body. Everyone has their own biases and, as long as they are aware of the choices, can make a rational decision.

Fish is another conundrum. Doubtlessly fish oil is a health boon, but it is not without its negative side. Modern commercial fishing is not only depleting fish stocks worldwide but also has unpleasant side effects of killing by-catch and spreading refuse in the ocean; farmed fish produces the attendant problems more commonly associated with other animal protein production lines such as crowding, pollution, and overuse of antibiotics. But there are certain things which are undeniably ethical choices: buying "dolphin-safe" tuna; following the yearly advice from sources such as the Monterey Bay Aquarium; and eating locally, reputably sourced fish and shellfish.

Ethical eating acknowledges that any awareness, and action taken upon it, is a positive step in the right direction. Consumerism is the driving force of our economy; it makes sense that our choices of what we buy can make an impact. A huge success story on this front is the organic-food movement in the U.S. Driven by consumer demand, it is the fastest-growing sector of the food industry. Is it best to have a garden and grow as much of your own food as possible? Yes, that is an excellent choice, but not available (or even desirable) to all.

Our "farm lunch" is thus named because, most of the time, we have greens from our garden and eggs from our chickens available. This can make you feel dangerously holier-than-thou. As lunch, it will keep you going strong all afternoon, but it is equally great for dinner. After living away at college, the kids actually come back and ask for it.

If you have a rice cooker, you can start the rice any time and then come back and do the rest after it is done (about 45 minutes). It's always an option to put some onion, garlic, salt, and olive oil in the rice cooker for a few minutes before adding the rice and water. A time-saving tip: cook rice in large quantities, and then store in fridge for later use.

## Farm Lunch

### Brown Rice with Sautéed Greens, Topped with a Fried Egg

PREP TIME (EXCLUDING RICE): 15 MINUTES

*How to sauté greens (greens options: kale, collards, swiss chard, arugula, spinach [in descending order of sturdiness]):*

*Start with a medium hot pan with olive oil, add any combination of finely chopped garlic/ginger/onions/shallots, and cook for a few minutes. Add greens in order of sturdiness—stems first, then tougher parts. Drizzle olive oil and liquid aminos (a healthy substitute for soy sauce) over the greens. Stir. Add tender leaves (spinach or any baby leaves) at very end—they just need less than 30 seconds on heat. Remove, and then fry an egg in the same pan.*

**Nutritional boost:** *add nutritional yeast on top*
**Spice boost:** *turmeric and black pepper*

I made a decision when I was about fifteen years old to become a vegetarian. You could say it was out of the blue, because no one else in my extended family or anyone I knew was a vegetarian. Or you could say it slowly arose from deep-seated convictions and experiences that, in retrospect, made it inevitable. Either way you look at it, I was aware then that my food choices impacted how I was going about the business of creating my life: I decided to not nourish myself on the suffering of animals.

My experience in veterinary school deepened my commitment to vegetarianism, as I learned firsthand the extremes to which factory farming had become big business in the U.S. But it also allowed me to intelligently advise others on how to make good "compromise" choices: if you do eat beef, choose pasture-fed, for feed lots comprise the majority of misery in cattle's life. If you eat eggs, make sure they are cage-free, so the hens aren't horribly confined; if you eat chicken, insist on antibiotic-free, as the unethical conditions in which most chickens are kept is tenable only by the routine feeding of antibiotics. Insist on organic milk or at least rBST-free milk for the same reason—if you can't give drugs at whim, then basic husbandry of the animals has to be of higher quality.

I have to admit that I would like to influence people to eat a more vegetarian-based diet. It just seems like such a no-brainer to me to do what is best for your health and the future of the planet—*and* is a more ethical choice, all at the same time. I have never been one to be strident about my choices—I recognize that food is a very personal part of this crazy journey of life. Attempting to convert a husband and raise three boys with my sensibilities about food has been enough of a challenge, but, if I often followed the child-rearing adage of "pick your fight," this is one I usually picked. And if I can, at this point in my life, share some of my accumulated wisdom on how to cook and eat to promote my values, I am game to do it.

## Breakfast Sandwich

### PREP TIME: 5 MINUTES

This fits the bill on so many levels—quick, healthy, doesn't require much packaging to go, and is an excellent replacement for fast-food biscuits. It even tastes good.

### Ingredients:
- ❏ *English muffins*
- ❏ *grated cheese*
- ❏ *egg*
- ❏ *spinach*

### Directions:
- ❏ *1. Heat skillet on medium high with 1 tbsp. butter*
- ❏ *2. Put muffin in toaster*
- ❏ *3. Crack an egg into skillet cook 2 minutes*
- ❏ *4. Flip egg and then put 1 tbsp. cheese and a few shredded leaves on top cook 2 minutes*
- ❏ *5. Remove muffin from toaster, and place on plate or reusable wrap*
- ❏ *6. Assemble*

***Spice boost:*** *cayenne pepper (cayenne is the main ingredient in most hot sauces and is cheaper and healthier than most of the processed alternatives)*
***Nutritional boost:*** *use multigrain unsweetened English muffins*

I haven't been a perfect vegetarian for thirty-five years. About five months into my first pregnancy, I experienced an irresistible urge to eat chicken. So I did—for a few months. I figured my body knew better than my brain about this growing-a-baby-thing. And later, when I was feeding three always-hungry boys who were no longer heeding my high-minded vegetarian mores, I periodically bought a "quarter-cow" from our local grass-fed purveyor. Having hunks of meat in the freezer was an anomaly for me, but the cows lived a nice life in a big green pasture and were taken to a nearby slaughterhouse. If we had to eat beef, this seemed to me a conscionable way to do it. The animals had a lovely life and a painless death. Who can ask for more?

**Rebecca's take:** Oddly enough, I had a similar experience. When I was pregnant with my first daughter, after being a vegetarian for fourteen years, I inexplicably begged my husband to make some herb-rubbed veal chops. Of all things.

*Beef Jerky*

PREP TIME: 20 MINUTES

*Slice a shoulder or rump roast as thinly as you can. Marinate in teriyaki sauce overnight. Lay pieces flat on a baking sheet, and cook about 4 hours at 200 degrees, flipping once.*

Although "falling off the wagon" is not something I am proud of, I recognize that exhaustion of willpower had a lot to do with it. In 2011, I mustered up the time and money to go to a yoga teacher training I had been eyeing for years. The fare was 100 percent healthy vegetarian for those sixteen days, and I was able to short-track myself back onto my chosen food path. I am again comfortable with what I nourish myself on.

One lesson learned—don't beat yourself up about your food choices. It is unproductive. Do the best you can—it will be enough.

# CHAPTER V

# PLANNING MEALS A WEEK AT A TIME

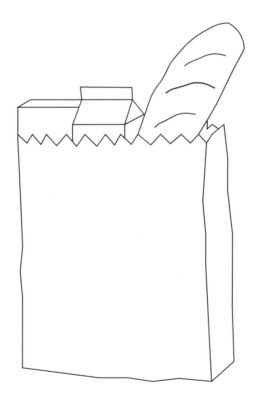

*Finding creativity from all corners of the globe*

The idea is to get going with a theme and get creative from there; it's like picking a basic beat and then riffing on it. It is also about taking the pressure off of making something new from scratch every night. Buy some basics, make a couple of complementary recipes, and mix and match from there. One great relief as a mother was when I would ask what my child wanted for lunch, and he would say "ant's picnic," which meant that I, with him helping, would assemble a group of yummy finger foods (for a toddler on a very large plate or segmented plate so they weren't touching!). An example would be a few grapes, several peanuts, 1 piece of string cheese, a turkey roll (1 slice deli turkey rolled up), ½ piece whole-wheat toast, and a carrot stick. Something about this just seemed so easy. I have tried to incorporate this idea into the following guidelines for weekly meal (lunch and dinner) plans by using finger foods to spice up the menu.

# MIDDLE EASTERN

For a healthy vegetarian week, make hummus (see recipe on p. 62) and tabbouleh, which store beautifully in the fridge. Also buy the following to add variety:

*Dried apricots, almonds, goat cheese, fava beans, salad greens, and pita bread*

### Pita Toast

*Cut pitas in half, and then split open, spray with olive oil, sprinkle with Greek seasoning (can buy or use basil and oregano) or Za'atar (thyme, oregano, and marjoram mixture); sprinkle with a little parmesan cheese and then broil for 4 minutes.*

### Tabbouleh

Some tabbouleh has more grain than vegetable; some is very parsley-heavy. Experiment and see what you like best, or just do it differently every time! If you keep the "base" in the fridge, you can make a different version every night.

*Make the base: Combine 2 cups bulghur wheat, 2½ cups boiling water, and 1 tbsp. salt in a glass bowl, cover, and let sit for 20 minutes. Then add ½ cup lemon juice and ½ cup olive oil. Chill in the fridge. Later, add whatever of the following you have and/or like: parsley, mint, carrots, cucumbers, tomatoes, olives, feta cheese, scallions.*

# SOUTH AMERICAN

These are my personalized healthy versions of recipes I have enjoyed on my travels in various South American countries. Can always add beef to feel Argentine.

*Grate raw carrots, and marinate with equal parts olive oil and apple-cider vinegar, enough to lightly coat carrots. Use salt, pepper, and celery seed to spice, as desired.*

*Boil quartered new potatoes until soft; drain and cool. Hard boil eggs, and then peel and cut into chunks. Mix the dressing: olive oil, apple-cider vinegar, Dijon, finely minced garlic and onion, salt and pepper. Combine all together. Options to add: fresh basil, sunflower seeds, chopped celery.*

*Cut 20 oz. whitefish into ½ cm cubes, and marinate in 1 cup lime juice in glass, covered container in refrigerator at least 1 hour. Add diced purple onion, parsley, salt, and crushed red pepper.*

## *Shrimp Bruschettini*

**PREP TIME: 30 MINUTES**

You can make the mash and store it; then just make daily portions with already-cooked shrimp. (I promise you, you'll eat double the number of these you think you will!)

*Mash 2 avocados with 1 tbsp. lime juice, 1 tbsp. sea salt, and 2 tbsp. sriracha mayonnaise. Spread on bruschettini (or any toasted bread round); then put 1 cooked shrimp on top.*

# SPANISH

Sometimes it feels like tapas is the most inviting way to eat. Everything here but the salad can be made ahead and is easily reheated. Add bread to your shopping list; then add any cured meats you desire and Manchego cheese for an "ant's picnic" smorgasbord throughout the week.

## *Tortilla*

**COOK TIME: 30 MINUTES**

*Cook 1 potato (cut into very small pieces) and 1 onion in your 10" cast-iron pan with olive oil and salt until potato is done. Add 1 cup peas (fresh or frozen); then add 8 beaten eggs (for 10" pan). Turn heat down to low, and let slowly cook from the bottom up. When there is only about ½ cm. loose (uncooked) egg left on top, pop into the oven to broil for a few minutes. Turn out onto a large, flat plate and serve in pie-shaped pieces.*

## *Arugula Salad*

**PREP TIME: 15 MINUTES**

*Place arugula and goat cheese in salad bowl. Heat ⅓ cup of pine nuts or walnuts in about ¼ cup of olive oil and 1 tsp. sea salt; then pour over lettuce. Mix with juice of 1 lemon.*

**COOK TIME: 20 MINUTES**

*Fry 1 bulb of thickly sliced garlic in canola or grapeseed oil (enough to cover the pan) and coarse sea salt on medium heat. Once the garlic is brown and crispy, add shrimp to the pan, and cook, turning once, until both sides turn pink. Sprinkle juice of ½ a lemon, and add red-pepper flakes to taste.*

**PREP TIME: 5 MINUTES**

*Cut 1 head of cauliflower into slices about 1 cm. thick. Coat with olive oil, pepper, and salt. Lay flat on a cookie sheet, and cook for 25 minutes at 350 degrees, turning once halfway through.*

# INDIAN

Make a big pot of rice of your choice. Buy a package of *naan* at the grocery store and make the Vegetable Curry—see recipe on (p. 43) and the following salad and *raita* for a sauce and you have days' worth of satisfying lunches and dinners.

**PREP TIME: 30 MINUTES**

*Stir-fry onion, garlic, and ginger in olive oil in a saucepan. Add salt and black pepper (curry powder optional); then add 3 cups of boiling water and 1½ cups dry lentils. Cook until tender, about 20 minutes. Cool; then add lime zest and juice of ½ lime. Add vegetables of your choice (you can vary it throughout the week): cilantro, parsley, peppers, kale or swiss chard, carrots, cooked potatoes.*

### Raita

**PREP TIME: 5 MINUTES**

*Mix plain yogurt with chopped cucumber for a cooling topping on any Indian food*

# ITALIAN

Buy some Italian bread at the store and make the following recipes to send yourself some Mediterranean vibes.

### Pasta al Pesto

**PREP TIME: 20 MINUTES**

*Chop about 1 cup mixed parsley, basil, and/or arugula. Put in bottom of large bowl with 1 tsp. sea salt, ¼ cup parmesan, 4 tbsp. butter and/or olive oil, and 1-3 minced clove(s) garlic (how much raw garlic one prefers is highly variable!). Cook 1 box of your favorite pasta (I love bowtie with this because the sauce gets stuck in all the crevices), drain, dump in bowl, and stir.*

### Mediterranean Salad

**PREP TIME: 20 MINUTES**

*Mix 1 box gemelli or penne pasta (cooked) with tomatoes, purple onion, parsley, minced garlic, ½ cup olive oil, ¼ cup lemon juice or vinegar, and 2 cans cannellini beans.*

**Antipasto**

PREP TIME: 5 MINUTES

*This one is so simple! Just lay out an appetizing amount of buffalo mozzarella, olives, salami, and roasted peppers to fit your crowd. If you want to go rustic, put it on a cutting board and serve with breadsticks, focaccia, or whatever you've got that works.*

**Bruschetta**

PREP TIME: 15 MINUTES

*Dice Roma tomatoes, and mix with chopped fresh basil and olive oil, salt, and balsamic vinegar. Spread on toasted Italian or French bread rounds.*

# CHAPTER VI
# YOU ARE WHAT YOU EAT

*Make food and the creation of meals an integral part of a healthy lifestyle*

For those of us who attended public schools in the '70s and '80s, the ubiquitous "You are what you eat" posters are indelibly marked in our brains, alongside the "food pyramids." And at this moment in the twenty-first century, we don't have to establish a link between food choices and health; there is a mountain of information pointing toward that particular truth. Our job is the converse—to wade through the plethora of information for you and give the down-and-dirty on what's in and what's out. Misinformation also abounds, and research is constantly evolving, but we can stand by a few things based on both our experience and the cultural and biological history of humanity.

Food is a fractal of life. For example, take the concept of diversity, which has been shown to benefit everything, from the classroom, to buying stocks, to choosing a team, to making decisions in the boardroom. As I consider the discrete uses of various types of oils, or advise buying rice, oat and coconut flours, or recommend trying goat- and sheep-milk cheeses to avoid a sole reliance on cow's milk, I recognize that it is really pretty simple: the more diverse our food choices are, the more likely they are healthier. Following are lists to help you vary your sources of common foodstuffs. As a disclaimer, of course, some people have allergies, so follow your doctor's advice on those products. And take manufacturers' sometimes confusing health claims with a grain of salt. The best you can do is be informed and experiment.

## Diversity Lists:

### CHEESES
- Cow—if not organic could have pharmaceutical residues
- Goat—feta for example, great on salads
- Sheep—yummy Manchego is of ovine origin
- Vegan—if you're vegan . . .

### OILS
- Olive—use extra virgin for salads, regular for sautéing over medium heat
- Sesame—so tasty for Asian cooking
- Canola—good for baking

- Coconut—for frying, conflicting evidence to its health benefits; maybe the jury is still out on this one
- Grapeseed—excellent multi-use

**FLOURS**

- Wheat—buy unbleached (Google dioxin—or just trust me: you don't want it in your food)
- Whole wheat—definitely changes taste for baking, substitute carefully
- Oat—easy to make in coffee grinder from oatmeal; can substitute for ½ of the called-for flour in most recipes with no accommodation
- Rice—gluten-free, changes texture of baked goods
- Coconut—imparts a sweetish, coconutty (!) taste
- Spelt—a genetic variety of wheat; good partial substitute
- Gluten-Free—can buy blends that are really good but expensive, too
- Almond—can use small amounts in substitution

**SALTS**

- Pink—supposedly healthiest
- Lite—potassium salt, so low sodium
- Sea—coarse or fine granules; most delicious
- Iodized—with Iodine, an essential nutrient; good idea to use sometimes

**MILKS**

- Dairy (cow)—buy organic
- Almond—can have a lot of sugar added
- Soy—conflicting advice about its health benefits; may be best to stick to fermented form of soy, for example, tofu
- Rice—kind of bland, if you ask me
- Oat—if you like oats, try it
- Coconut—it tastes like, well, coconut!!
- Goat—an excellent alternative to dairy if you like the distinct taste

### GRAINS

- Couscous—quick and easy
- Quinoa—try it; you may not like it
- White Rice—so good and so, well, white
- Brown Rice—if you can learn to love it, then go for nutty
- Wild Rice—for those who like diversity, throw some in to any other rice you are cooking
- Barley—great in soups
- Farro—the "in" grain
- Bulghur—for tabbouleh

In addition to diversity being a healthy certainty, I certainly believe age-old wisdom that recurs across different cultures is seldom wrong. An example of this is fermented foods. They are common in many cultures—think tofu (Japan), sauerkraut (Germany), and kim chee (Korea), to name a few. You could add in wine and beer, but I won't go there for the purposes at hand! The recent *kombucha* craze piggybacks on the idea of healthful benefits from fermentation, and there may be some truth to it.

Spices are another ubiquitous facet of cooking across cultures. Rather than debating the controversial details about the particular health benefits of specific spices, let's just say that, across the board, they provide palatability to food that reduces the need for unhealthier ways to make food delicious! Use as much as possible. My go-tos:

- Turmeric and black pepper (Indian)
- Celery seed and thyme (Italian)
- Oregano and basil (Greek)
- Ginger and garlic (Asian)
- Salt and pepper (American)
- Cayenne and chili powder (Mexican)
- Thyme, oregano, and marjoram (Middle Eastern)
- Fresh herbs: use in almost any combination; hard to go wrong
- *Gomasio*: a mixture of sea salt, sesame seed, and seaweed (Japanese)

Sometimes I will think to myself, *Have I eaten a curry in the last week or so?* Have you? If not, make yourself one. Your body will thank you. Here is an easy way to reap the benefits of millennia of Indian wisdom.

**Curry**

PREP TIME: 15 MINUTES

COOKING TIME: 45 MINUTES

*Sauté onions, garlic, ginger, potatoes, and carrots in olive oil with salt and curry powder. After 5 minutes or so, add 1 can of coconut milk. Simmer for about 30 minutes; then add any other vegetables you like and/or tofu or shrimp (if using raw shrimp, make sure sauce is at a low boil before adding) and cook for about 10 minutes more. Serve over rice.*

Food fads are common; currently paleo and vegan are pretty popular. Remember, there can be healthful benefits to cutting just about anything out of our modern-day diet, so don't get too caught up in the latest trend. But these two certainly have their benefits, with some science behind them. There is no question that easing your body's digestive load is good for it. I came up with this paleo-vegan recipe that is a pretty tough combination to make delicious. But for me, basically anytime there is a perfectly ripe avocado involved, I consider it a meal. Breakfast, lunch, dinner—no matter: this one can fill the bill anytime. Time-saving tip: Bake 4-5 sweet potatoes at a time, and store extras in fridge.

**Meal of Champions**

PREP TIME: 10 MINUTES

*Fry an already baked, skinned, and cubed sweet potato for about 5 minutes in coconut oil. Serve in a dish with ½ an avocado sliced in it and a handful of blueberries.*

**Nutritional boost:** *add a fried egg (not vegan anymore!)*

*__Calorie boost:__ add 2 slices whole wheat bread (my favorite: Ezekiel Raisin toasted—not paleo anymore!)*

*__Spice tip:__ turmeric and cayenne*

Another way to reimagine your methods of cooking to make them healthier is to incorporate the following:

## Healthy Condiments

- Tamari—use as soy-sauce substitute for all Asian cooking
- Liquid Aminos—use as soy-sauce substitute for sautéing vegetables
- Nutritional Yeast—sprinkle on any grains
- Mustard—add into dressings

## Health Boosts

- Chia and flax seeds: I grind them up in a coffee grinder (the whole seeds are just the right size to annoyingly stick in your teeth!) and then store them airtight in the fridge. They'll last for weeks.
- Raw sunflower, pumpkin seeds, and chopped almonds: Mix and store in airtight container, close at hand, so you can toss some on cereal or yogurt.
- Wheat germ—sprinkle on yogurt.

## Taste Boosts

- Lemon zest—grated lemon peel adds intense flavor to any dish such as baked goods, seafood, or salads
- Toasted nuts—pine, walnut, pecan, or pistachio are all great additions to salads or grains.
- Honey, agave, and maple syrup—my favorite sweeteners, all-natural, use moderately.

Making vegetables the mainstay of the meal is a simple way to eat healthy; with this recipe, it's easy to apportion the largest part of your plate to the veggies.

## *Roasted Vegetables*

**PREP TIME: 15 MINUTES**

**COOKING TIME: 60 MINUTES**

*Mix about 6 cups assorted winter/root vegetables (potatoes, sweet potatoes, Brussels sprouts, parsnips, beets, carrots) in a bowl, and toss with olive oil, balsamic vinegar, and sea salt. Optionally, add sliced onions and garlic, and/or season with fresh rosemary. Roast in 350-degree oven for 45-60 minutes (depending on how small the pieces are).*

I am thankful for memories of my maternal grandparents' wholesome relationship with food—most reminiscences resonate around their gardens, orchards, and meals. The sound of an orange-juice squeezer sends me right back to Bama S's kitchen; to this day, I never order apple pie because it's always a disappointment compared to the ones she baked with their home-grown, perfectly tart apples. Swiss chard and cherry tomatoes that Papa S harvested an hour before dinner were delicious treats even to a young child. And the healthy consequences have been passed down through the generations.

The following recipe chronicles the changes in the way I think about food. Over the years, white sugar gives way to honey, milk can become soy or almond milk, white flour becomes half whole wheat, and margarine is definitely out. When I make this recipe today, I use organic bananas, canola oil, honey, free-range eggs, almond milk, an aluminum-free baking powder, and a mixture of oat and gluten-free flour.

Cooking will always be something which is passed on from generation to generation, but as knowledge increases about what our bodies need and our environment is impacted by our activities, our recipes for food and health will evolve.

Throwing it back to the Catskill Mountains near New York City, my atypical Jewish grandmother was obsessed with healthy eating. My earliest memories of her include her hovering over my bowl of hot cereal or yogurt, sprinkling wheat germ and slicing bananas into the bowl in real-time. She read *Prevention* magazine cover-to-cover and preached. We teased her, but she was absolutely adorable. Some things she had quite right: you need protein, fresh fruit, leafy greens, and not too much sugar. Other lessons were less supported by data, such as "we don't drink until after we've eaten, or it washes down the vitamins." Her zeal for the healthy and the wholesome set up the perfect dynamic with my grandfather. He would sneak us kids down to the Dairy Queen for banana splits, and we'd love it more because it felt forbidden. It's only after parenting two kids that it occurs to me that she probably knew all along.

For me, healthy eating is a matter of values that I associate with family. We've had some devastating losses and some valiant cancer battles, a few of them triumphant. I don't take good health for granted, and I hope I've passed that along to my kids. It's something to be grateful about when you have it but also something to actively strive for, and a diverse diet is project number one to get you there.

## Rebecca's Bowl

**PREP TIME: 20-40 MINUTES**

- ❏ Fried Egg
- ❏ Red Quinoa
- ❏ Cubed and shredded veggies
- ❏ *Sriracha*

*The bowl craze had me ordering in way too often. There's just no reason for that. You can throw in whatever's in the fridge, sauté and mandolin a few veggies, and fry one perfect egg, and you've got the best food there is. Cook the quinoa (or rice or couscous) as you normally would. Heat up a tbsp. of olive oil (or sesame or avocado or sunflower oil) with some combination of chopped onion, garlic, and shallot. Once those are translucent and you can smell them, start adding the vegetables in order of thickness. If you want more of an Asian flavor, try some* tamari *and citrus juices. Fry the egg in the "matching"* *flavor, whatever you choose. At the last minute, drizzle some* sriracha *on top—or let your* *diners do it to their own taste.*

## A Note About Organics

There are many articles out there on the topic of when you should really try to hold out for organic and when you can probably buy conventional without losing sleep or money. Of course, this presumes some privilege—and that should be called out right away. There are many who may not even see these as options and plenty of people who do not grow their own organic produce or live close to a place that grows or sells it—in fact, probably the majority of Americans. However, when you unpack it, we're all invested in our own health and welfare and that of our children, so to the extent that we have a choice or want to know more about how to evaluate the proposition, here are some quick rules of thumb that I use.

### *Organic*

Whatever grows underground, especially if you eat the skin.

Things that get sprayed a lot because they are delicate.

Such as: potatoes, strawberries, apples, stonefruits, spinach, lettuce, and cucumbers.

### *Don't Panic*

Relatively thick skin that you don't consume.

Such as: bananas, avocados, eggplant, grapefruit, and oranges.

# CHAPTER VII

# REAL QUESTIONS, REAL ANSWERS

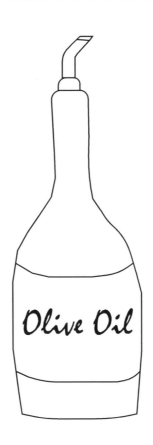

*"Hey, mom: How do I . . . ?"*

These are some things that are bound to come up. We know that because they did. As our two eldest move through their early twenties, they are full of questions when it comes to running their own kitchens. We try our best to provide answers with humor, patience, and love.

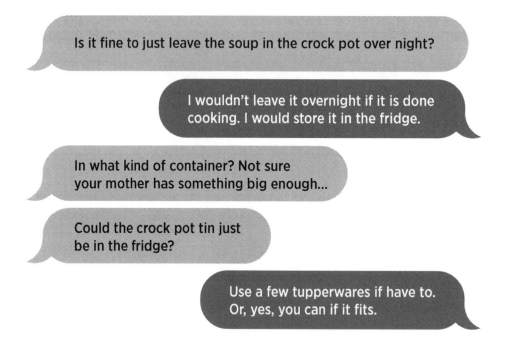

One thing this conversation is missing is the warning that storing food within a few hours or even sooner is the safest way to go. If left out longer than that, bacteria can form that actually might make someone sick.

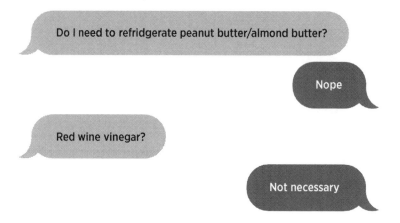

That said, nut butters and vinegars can go in the refrigerator. Sometimes, if the nut butters have natural oils at the top, this may be preferable at least until they are more absorbed into the more solid part of the butter. Vinegar is almost indestructible, but it's probably best not to keep it in direct sunlight.

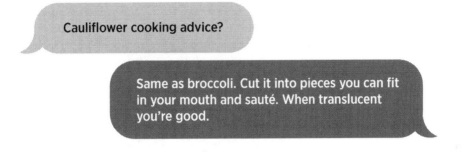

**Cauliflower cooking advice?**

**Same as broccoli. Cut it into pieces you can fit in your mouth and sauté. When translucent you're good.**

A fun recent craze is "ricing" the cauliflower. Just food-process the cut-and-cleaned pieces to the desired texture. They can then be steamed, stir-fried, or cooked pretty much any way you'd cook bigger pieces. It's faster than actual rice and lower in carbohydrates. Another delicious way to cook it is with breadcrumbs, parmesan, pepper, and olive oil—baking it at 375 degrees for about 20 minutes works out great.

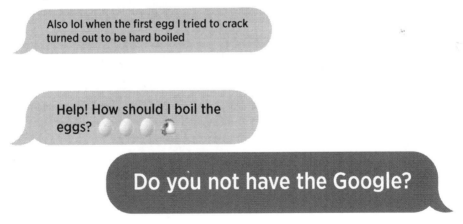

**Also lol when the first egg I tried to crack turned out to be hard boiled**

**Help! How should I boil the eggs?** 🥚🥚🥚 🐣

**Do you not have the Google?**

Sometimes you've just got to cut the apron strings. However, one less well-documented trick is that peeling eggs is easier if you put them in cold water after you take them off the stove and add a dash of vinegar.

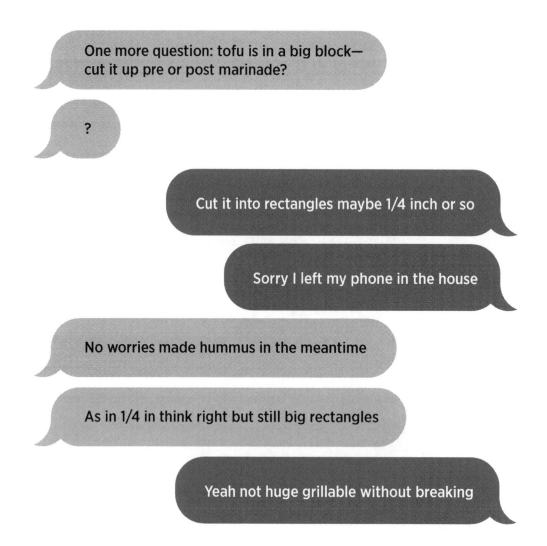

One more question: tofu is in a big block—cut it up pre or post marinade?

?

Cut it into rectangles maybe 1/4 inch or so

Sorry I left my phone in the house

No worries made hummus in the meantime

As in 1/4 in think right but still big rectangles

Yeah not huge grillable without breaking

The surface of tofu takes on the flavor of the marinade in a pronounced way. Cutting it before cooking means more surface area—simple as that. It grills beautifully on a panini maker. It really looks like you tried.

Oh shit! I didn't realize it was big cous cous? Did it cook ok?

Usually that you would cook more like Pasta—I didn't realize

Oops well it cooked great

But the tofu looks yummy. How about a little green spinach?

As long as it tastes good! How's the tofu?

Super good

Did cinnamon, garlic, lemon, olive oil, honey, and apple cider vinegar

Fancy! sounds yummy

Super yummy

Couscous comes in different sizes. Pouring hot broth over the smaller grain is a fast, easy way to cook it. Here, my daughter was using either Israeli or Lebanese couscous, which is really more like small pasta pearls. I generally cook it and drain it the way I would pasta and then possibly sauté it in the pan with whatever flavor and ingredients profile I'm using. But here, it all worked out and cooked well enough, apparently.

Panini-maker grilled tofu. Speaks for itself.

Cinnamon tofu with cranberry couscous!

Recipe for Italian wedding soup says 8 hrs—actually take that long?

Never made it so I don't know! Is that crock pot?

Yeah

Then maybe

Slow-cookers have rules all their own. If you're using them, look up the cooking times!

> Spinach that has a sell by date of today still good? Has lots of condensation inside the container.

> Should be ok but smell it and look for wilting and slime if you are worried.

Sell dates say what they say, and condensation doesn't mean much. Vegetables are bad if they look or smell bad or have changed in texture. That's that.

> NYC baby all good stuff is expensive

> But 17 dollars for a small size juice and small sandwich? that's pushing it a little

> Yeah maybe but Palo Alto is the same

> true

Nothing says, "Cook your way to independence" quite like the prices at a bougie juice bar.

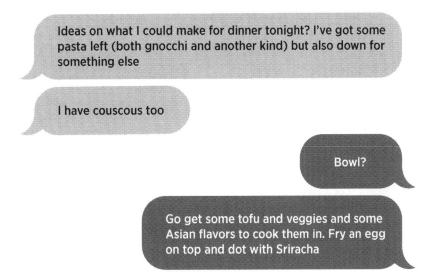

> Ideas on what I could make for dinner tonight? I've got some pasta left (both gnocchi and another kind) but also down for something else

> I have couscous too

> Bowl?

> Go get some tofu and veggies and some Asian flavors to cook them in. Fry an egg on top and dot with Sriracha

If you are at a loss about what to make for dinner, start with what you have. Pick your protein or your carb, and build around it accordingly. If you're lucky enough to live near a local market, you can always grab that one missing ingredient, and you're there.

Too much salt is hard to fix. The best thing to do is increase the volume of the other main ingredients if you have them, even if you don't have them all.

Too much heat is a problem that is similar to too much salt, so increasing the proportions is one fix, but adding something sweet can counteract some of the overpowering spice.

> I am sauteing random vegetables. How do I start?

> A few tablespoons of olive oil, some minced garlic and/or shallot or onion. Translucent, don't burn them!

If you're cooking by the seat of your pants, you really can't go wrong with some basic flavors like olive oil, garlic, onion, or shallot. At the very least, the kitchen is going to start to smell good.

> What do I do to not screw up the rice?

> If it's in a pot do NOT take the top off. If you're using a rice cooker it is pretty idiot proof unless your measurements are way off!

Cooking rice is all about steam, so keeping the lid on for the prescribed time really does make a difference. Rice cookers seem to know things they've been programmed to know, but wildly imprecise measurements are still not an easy save.

# CHAPTER VIII
# FOOD IS FUEL

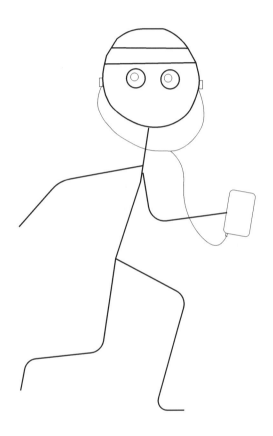

*Good food can get you to your goals*

Food is full of cultural associations, all worthy of analysis and celebration. But, most elementarily, food is fuel for bodies in motion and minds at work. What and when you eat have implications for how you feel as well as for how you perform.

When I became a vegetarian/sometime pescatarian, it was a practical decision. In parallel with Shelley, I was about fifteen years old. But Shelley's journey was more soulful than mine. I had grown up with the staple of family holidays being things like roast chicken and brisket and never thought much about it until I began training hard as a cross-country and marathon runner. Once that became a focus of my days, I began to notice that I simply didn't digest meat as well as other foods. That was a hard thing to reckon with at mile six of a twelve-mile run. So, I cut it out because my single-minded goal was to be a better runner.

Red meat wasn't at all hard to give up, and parting with chicken proved pretty easy, too. I ate fish only occasionally anyway, so that stayed on the roster. Once I went to college, overachieving eating hang-ups began to manifest. I started to make rules, which, in retrospect, were ways to avoid fat and calories, but I believed them to be about personal standards. So, I'd skip the ice cream and just eat the cone or limit myself to foods in the dining hall that had no more than three ingredients. By then, cutting out animal proteins was a habit, and the mystery meat served *en masse* didn't exactly tempt me to break it. I stuck to salads, simple carbs like pasta and rice, whole grains, and legumes. I ran far and relatively fast and took up martial arts, working out at 5:00 a.m. every morning. My diet kept me going, hang-ups and all.

## A Note About Raising Strong Women

The relationship between mothers and daughters is at the heart of every matter for me. I was a big tomboy growing up, two brothers and one sister, all about sports and '80s unisex fashion. I had my first child, a girl, very easily. My second, also a girl, came after a secondary infertility struggle and a number of painful miscarriages. She was a twin, and we lost her brother early in the second trimester. A journey that was full of unexpected turns made me the mom of girls, and it's been the most challenging, rewarding, stress-inducing, joy-dripping, values-testing experience I have ever had.

To raise a young woman is daunting. I thought hard and read every book I could find. I tried to revive Ophelia and keep the Queen Bees from stinging. The messages they get in this crazy, plugged-in world are dizzying: Be smart, beautiful, confident, fit, compassionate, loving, intuitive, charming, bad-ass. It's exhausting. Here's what I go for in the end: you are important, and you matter. You are what you are, and what you are is enough. So simple. So complicated.

One thing I've worked really hard on is that my girls have a positive relationship with food. Sounds easy enough—just sling the hash with a smile, and they'll equate food with nurturing, right? Ha! They see it all—the one-food diets, the "I'm a vegan because my waist has gotten smaller since I decided to be vegan," the "I eat only on weekends," the "my mom has to bring me an *acai* bowl before practice—it's the only thing I like," the airbrushing, posting, "like"-mongering—and all of it is about women's bodies in the end. What does it mean to be "hot?" As my older daughter recently wrote in a piece that my younger daughter turned into a dance video, "The object of envy of all the girls, fought over by all the boys—that is what it means to be pretty." Ouch. My girls know that there's a connection between what they put inside them and how they feel as well as how they appear on the outside. And they want to feel great and perform well mentally and physically while looking good. No point in denying that, so best to cultivate and celebrate healthy choices whenever possible.

**A note from Shelley:** Speaking as someone with a history of mild anorexia, it helps me immeasurably to think of food as fuel for my body and mind. It simplifies it. Takes away the baggage. It serves *me* (not the other way around, as so often happens in eating disorders, where food rules your life).

Hummus with *harissa*, cucumbers, carrots, and whole-wheat pita is the best after-school snack for my athlete. She has no time, has to attack her homework, and then hit the dance studio for hours every day. I blend the hummus fresh.

## Hummus

PREP TIME: 15 MINUTES

*One can of drained garbanzo beans, 2 tbsp. of tahini, 4 tbsp. of olive oil, juice of 3 lemons, 1 tsp. each of salt, pepper, and paprika. Just blend. Keeps refrigerated for about a week. Then drizzle in the harissa at the last minute, toast up some pita on the panini maker, and peel and chop the carrots and cucumber. It takes 5-10 minutes, and it is the best thing ever to give her energy, all the food groups, and the ability to work out at a high level after an exhausting day of school and stress.*

My girls like their grains. They aren't satisfied with just a salad for dinner.

## Couscous Variations

PREP TIME: 15 MINUTES

*Couscous is absurdly easy to make. Just pour hot broth over it, and cover for 15 minutes (add nuts, fruit, chopped veggies as you wish) Fluff with a fork. You can make your own broth base and add water, or grab some organic bouillon if you don't have a carton of broth. I use low-sodium vegetable broth when I don't have time or the ingredients to make it myself; it keeps really well in the fridge for months on end.*

## Lemon Pasta with Asparagus

PREP TIME: 20 MINUTES

*I've shown my kids that pasta doesn't have to be heavy and carby. Whole-wheat or spinach noodles are really good, especially with a nice light lemon sauce. Just do equal parts lemon juice and olive oil, a little bit of garlic, salt, pepper, and maybe oregano or parsley, if you're into that. Then, roast some thick-cut zucchini or some asparagus with a touch of balsamic glaze, and you have a delicious vegetarian meal. For protein, white cannellini beans are great and easy to add. Expert tip: undercook the pasta by a minute, and then sauté it in a pan with the veggies and sauce. It sticks to the noodles, and everything blends. Worth washing the pan over.*

## Food and Feminism

I never think of cooking as a shackle or a limit. To me, it is a fundamental life skill. If you have the ability to gather ingredients and feed yourself, you are well on your way to being strong and independent. When I met my husband, we were both law students—equals engaged in similar activity. We began with the rules that if one cooked, the other cleaned, or we just did it all together. When we started our crazy careers, it was more like whoever got home first was the cook—we kept it simple, with mostly vegetables as well as rice – and pasta-based foods. For example, there was a handmade pasta shop near our apartment. We'd keep pumpkin ravioli in the freezer, cook it up with spinach or escarole, and call it dinner. Actually, for the first six months that I worked, he was still in school for a master's, and I came home to a beautifully prepared meal every night (if I made it home in time for dinner at all, which I often did not).

Since our kids arrived, I have done more of the cooking, but that's because I work from home, have taken breaks, and reinvented my career. Also, I like it! For us, there's never been a wrangle on the topic of division of labor. We each do what we want to do and work together to make the best contributions we can to our family. I know I'm extraordinarily fortunate in this regard, but because of the way things have always been, I worry very little about my female children being hemmed in by what they might perceive to be societally imposed gender roles. Instead, I see teaching them to cook and run a kitchen as empowerment. No different than driving, doing laundry, sewing (which I am terrible at, but my husband is excellent!), or knowing a thing or two about self-defense. I hope my daughters never feel that they have to rely on someone else to do these things for them. They are capable!

# CHAPTER IX
# HIJACKED BY OXYTOCIN

*Culinary insights from the trenches of motherhood*

Not to be confused with the oft-abused prescription opioid oxycontin, oxy*tocin* is a naturally occurring neuropeptide that has been nicknamed the "love drug." It was so "in" a few years ago that even Nicholas Kristof wrote an op-ed in the *New York Times* about it. I experienced its effects firsthand with childbirth. Previously being a sensible woman, I became a baby-food-making, bread-baking, health-food nut. I gravitated toward becoming the "Earth Mother" as naturally as a duck takes to water (as I overheard my husband telling an acquaintance soon after the birth of our first child). The natural compassion I had always felt for animals multiplied at the sight of my newborn, and I was smitten. Mostly working part time, I spent a lot of time in the kitchen with my children, as baking and soup-making felt like productive things to do when confined to the house. My older boys both attended a Montessori school for a time, and I learned from those classrooms the importance of having children do it themselves. My studies and my experiences had already stressed the importance of healthy food, and I ratcheted my standards up even more for nourishing my children.

**Rebecca's note:** When we started this book, even I mistakenly thought that my dear friend and old roommate was making a brave and honest confession about her struggle with *oxycontin* to our readers—a struggle I had not heard about. And I loved and respected her for it. And told her so. She was understandably confused.

Being the mother of three boys has indelibly shaped my life. I consciously attempted to be gender-neutral in their upbringing. But I realized, through careful observation of boys conducted from the moment my first child emerged with a penis, that boys either played their pretend and fun games with balls or with guns. Being solidly anti-gun, anti-violence, and anti-hunting, I immediately went from being pretty anti-athletics to carrying variously shaped balls around with me wherever I went (that was somewhat of a success insofar as all my boys became avid soccer players). They had dolls and a fabulous wooden dollhouse, we performed puppet shows, and we cooked together. Going to the grocery store was an opportunity to increase a toddler's vocabulary as to shapes, colors, and foods. I was the mom who encouraged high-chair messiness and was a disciple of *Pretend Soup*, a cookbook by Katzen and Henderson that encouraged children to cook. I was happy to let go of control in my kitchen—and standards of cleanliness—to foster their interest in food.

But as my kids got older, their interest waned, their free time shrunk, and their caloric needs increased—a perfect trifecta. Food production became an enormous sink of my time and energy. I learned that growing, athletic teenage boys consume enormous amounts of food, often. Living on a farm added to the difficulty—there was no running to get a quick bite somewhere. Cooking four meals a day from scratch, served on the proverbial platter, almost did me in. During a particularly difficult time, my parents gave me a gift of a cook, who, for a three-month period when my husband was traveling, would come to the house once a week and prepare three dinners and put them in the fridge.

I rued losing my young helpers in the kitchen and the companionship of cooking together. I was afraid I was becoming *that* mother of boys who runs herself into the ground so her children can thrive. The summer of 2016, I consciously tried to scale back my cooking for a while—we ate more take-out, and others did step up to the plate. Now, when I come back from work and someone asks me "What's for dinner?" I reply honestly, "I don't know!" and it's a small liberation.

My husband recently threw a small dinner party for my birthday. Two caterers showed up at the house and proceeded to serve the most delicious appetizers to us. When it was time to sit down for what was to be a scrumptious dinner, one of my friends added to the birthday toasts by saying, "And everything tastes better when cooked by a man." The two young men in the kitchen smiled, and all the guests laughed heartily. But perhaps no one appreciated the comment as deeply as I did.

But forget all the work and the angst—there is nothing that speaks more to comfort than homemade meals. There are times when it is worth the extra effort to produce wonders from the kitchen. If you can allow yourself to dive into your earthy, *hygge* (a hip Danish word for "creating a cozy home") side without overextending yourself, you will create enjoyment for yourself and for whomever you choose to cook for.

Fresh-off-the-griddle pancakes and crepes are impressive, but really so easy. The only real work is cleaning the dishes. Always a crowd-pleaser for picky young guests, and equally nourishing to the soul of a family, are Sunday-morning pancakes.

## Basic Pancake Recipe

PREP TIME: 10 MINUTES

- ❑ *1 egg*
- ❑ *1 cup almond milk*
- ❑ *1 cup flour*
- ❑ *½ tsp. baking powder*

- ❑ *¼ tsp. salt*
- ❑ *Variations: add mashed banana, chopped pecans, chocolate chips, blueberries*

## Basic Crepe Recipe

PREP TIME: 10 MINUTES

- ❑ *1 egg*
- ❑ *1 cup almond milk*
- ❑ *½ cup flour*

*Pour about ½ of this into a crepe pan on low heat, and cook until very solid and flipable. Flip and cook on the other side, adding whatever you wish to the top at that time.*

*Savory:*

*Cheese, tomato, spinach, cooked potatoes, cooked egg, cooked vegetables, ham or turkey deli slices*

*Sweet:*

*Banana and Nutella*
*Strawberries and whipped cream*

What can be more symbolic of the Earth Mother than the wafting aroma of baking? I certainly succumbed to this lure as the ultimate nourishment for my children. My basic muffin recipe doesn't always come out the same. Living with this unknown, every time I start this process of baking, I return to a certain life lesson—we are not always in control. The chemical amalgamation of water, flour, and yeast (or baking powder) is somewhat magical. Perhaps I'm just not good enough to understand all the variables. Maybe I just *like* the surprise of creating something slightly different with each version. Sometimes the family "Oohs" and "Aahs" over the most scrumptious muffin they've ever tasted, and the dozen is gone in a few hours. Sometimes they diplomatically eat the breakfast that is served, maybe add a pat of butter and some jam, and seven or eight are put into the freezer before they mold. I will invariably eat those leftovers—usually the "healthy" take on this recipe.

## Basic Muffin Recipe

**PREP TIME (INCLUDING BAKING): 35 MINUTES**

*Combine wet ingredients in large bowl:*

- ❑ *2 eggs*
- ❑ *¾ cup canola oil*

- ❑ *½ cup brown sugar (substitute honey or ⅓ cup agave for more expensive but healthier version)*
- ❑ *1 tsp. vanilla*

*Sift together dry ingredients:*

- ❑ *2 cups flour\**
- ❑ *1 tsp. baking powder*

- ❑ *½ tsp. salt*

*Pour dry into wet, and gently stir. Then add one of the following options:*

- ❑ *1. 1 cup each grated zucchini and carrot, 1 tsp. cinnamon*
- ❑ *2. 2 mashed bananas, ½ cup pecans, ½ cup chocolate chips*

- ❑ *3. 1½ cups blueberries, 1 tbsp. lemon zest (grated peel)*
- ❑ *4. 1 mashed banana, ½ cup yogurt, ½ cup each dates and walnuts, ¾ cup oat bran soaked in ½ cup hot water*

*Pour into greased muffin tins (canola spray is easiest); bake 16-25 minutes at 350 degrees (time dependent upon your oven).*

*Note about flour: many gluten-free options exist, which you can substitute one-for-one. You can also mix white, whole-wheat, and/or oat flour with gluten-free options such as rice or coconut. You boost the nutrition, and sometimes the taste is even better. Experiment and see what you like (muffins are pretty fail-safe). Whatever flour you choose, buy organic and unbleached.*

**Time-saving tip:** *Preheat the oven first; then get all the ingredients together, make the batter, pop it in oven, and then do the cleanup. By the time you've finished, you'll have a delicious muffin to eat.*

For my second-favorite baking recipe, the title below says it all—it has been refined and reworked tens of times until I got this final version. I've adapted it to be higher protein, less sweet, and lower gluten than some traditional recipes. Serve toasted with honey butter as a dessert, or toast slices and make tomato and mayonnaise sandwiches. That's if there's any left over the next day.

Best Oatmeal Bread

In Bread mixing bowl:

Pour 2c. boiling water over 2c. old fashioned oats + 4 tbsp butter and 3 tsp salt.

Add 1/2 c. honey/molasses + 1 or 2 eggs

Dissolve 2 tbsp yeast in 1 c milk/water warm mixture

Add 6 1/2 c. flour (spelt/bread)

Knead 5 minutes, may need to add more flour (til dough stays on hook).

Rise in warm area, covered, for 1 hour. Transfer to 9x5" bread pans let rise until 1-2" above rim.

Bake 350° for 35/45 minutes, Cool on wire rack.

# CHAPTER X

# COMFORT FOOD

*Your body knows what it needs*

We've all eaten our feelings, and it shouldn't automatically be the cause of a shame spiral. Sometimes you just crave a certain something—a texture, a flavor, or a specific recipe because it reminds you of a simpler time or your original home. Food can be emotional and physical medicine—an elemental and pretty harmless way of finding your way back to equilibrium. Compared to the things people sometimes do when they are feeling "not quite right," breaking out an old recipe or whipping up a potion for that hacking cough seems pretty tame. But more than that, when you do it yourself, it's an act of empowerment. So, listen to your body and your inner child.

## Toast

Taking a minute to enjoy the simplest of things has benefits. If gratitude-journaling isn't your thing, try toast. Yup, toast. An amazing example of how turning up the heat can send something lackluster and ordinary in a dazzling, day-changing direction. Whatever bread you've got lying around—it can be a few days old or even frozen—you can make it a crispy, flavorful moment of comfort and inspiration. Mostly, I make toast on my panini maker, because I'm a sucker for light grill marks. Butter's great, but I like to change it up and go for olive oil or even avocado oil. Then, I usually sprinkle some fancy salt—pink or black makes me really happy. All of a sudden, it's a new day, and I'm Julia freaking Child. Or the kid whose mom just made her stomachache feel better. Homemade jams, fruit butters, or raw honey are other ways to make toast a party.

## Jelly Omelets

My grandfather wore a few hats—he was a teacher and a camp owner/director, and he co-owned a dairy with his brothers. They supplied many of the storied Catskill Mountain hotels with butter and eggs. So my grandparents' house was consequently long on eggs. And cooking them right was pretty sacred. My grandfather won our hearts as soon as we could eat with forks by making thin omelets in a small round pan, slathering them with strawberry jelly, and rolling them up like crepes. Probably, this was the first food I ever thought of as a comfort food. It's so easy, simple, and delicious.

## Simple Side Salad

There's something about cold, crispy lettuce, the right proportion of tomato, red onion, cucumber, olive oil, and red-wine vinegar that makes you feel like you're doing what you're supposed to be doing. When you make salad at home, you tend to take the "kitchen sink" approach—whatever's in the fridge or the cupboard, you feel compelled to use, to make an "interesting" salad. Those barrier-breaking concoctions are great and, sometimes, even all the meal you need. But other times, you just want what you'd get at the pizza place without going out. And when you make it fresh yourself, it's a really excellent, satisfying back-to-basics move.

## Mashed/Smashed Potatoes

These days, you can do sweet, purple, fingerling, or new potatoes—so many choices. And you don't have to make it buttery if that's not your preference. Just boil, mash with healthy oil, and season your way. My oil of choice is olive, and I love pepper and salt, plain and simple. But you can go with garlic, thyme, chili powder, or whatever you feel like trying. The point is, mashed/smashed potatoes are delicious and smooth. They remind you of holidays and good times—they're special, but you can make them anytime.

## The Potion

I'm an asthma mom. Many sleepless nights, groggy mornings, and weeks of hacking coughs have taught me that most cough medicine doesn't really work. Based on some family lore, I devised this potion and have found it to be some inexact combination of comforting and effective, and that's good enough.

*Just grate about 3 tbsp. of fresh ginger. Add ¼ cup of raw honey and the juice of 4 lemons. Add 3 cups of water. Stir, heat, and serve.*

## Oatmeal

When I was a competitive distance runner, oatmeal was the only thing I could eat before a race. It never upset my stomach, but it felt like it gave me more energy than the average carb. So when I want delicious, reliable fuel for a long day or a big effort, I turn to oatmeal. I like my oatmeal chewy. I know some people prefer it creamy, and that's legitimate. But I want to see each oat, rolled or steel cut. I want the texture to remind me that eating it is good for me, but that doesn't mean it has to lack for taste. I boil the water for oatmeal with dried fruit already added and drizzle in honey, agave, or maple syrup. Then, I put the oats in with some cinnamon and let them simmer. Last, I pour a little bit of almond milk into the bowl and add a small handful of crunchy nuts and some fresh fruit—apples, bananas, plums, nectarines, and/or berries. It's usually breakfast, but it makes an awesome snack or dessert. One of those things that is totally satisfying.

## Chocolate-Chip Cookie Cake

Chocolate-chip cookies have always been the dessert I can't resist. When I was in middle school, my best friend and I pooled our lunch money and bought sixteen soft and chewy chocolate cookies from the cafeteria (they were a quarter, and we each had two dollars). And we ate eight each. I wasn't sorry then, and I'm still not. When I was thirty-one or thirty-two, I told my husband that I didn't want birthday cake anymore—I just wanted my favorite thing in cake form. And so it has been. The recipe is the same—you just cook it in a round cake pan for about thirty minutes. You won't be sorry, either.

# CHAPTER XI

# THE SWEETER
# SIDE OF LIFE

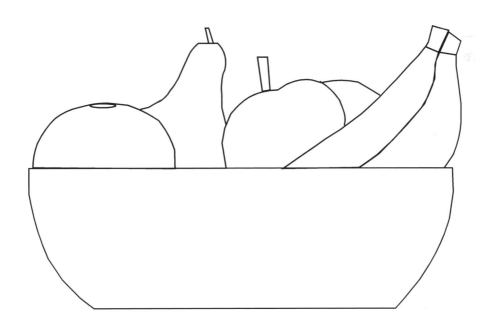

*Easy desserts, not too unhealthy*

Sometimes a few medjool dates and a handful of pecans (the perfect combination of sweet and chewy with rich and crunchy) with a peppermint tea is enough to satisfy a sweet tooth. Or you can try crumbling your favorite cookie (or two) into a bowl of yogurt, or pop a scoop of vanilla ice cream into a decaf coffee. When you have the time to go above and beyond, however, the recipes below will be sure to please.

### Baked Pear

**PREP TIME: 25 MINUTES**

*Core pear(s). Fill with granola, 1 tsp. maple syrup, and cinnamon. Bake until pear is soft, about 20 minutes at 350 degrees.*

### Shortcut Rice Pudding

**PREP TIME: 10 MINUTES**

Leftover rice is the best thing that can happen to a person. As long as that person has a food-safe source of heat.

*For a healthy, cheap dessert, I've taught my kids to warm up the leftover rice with some vanilla almond milk and then toss fresh berries over it. It's like fake rice pudding, without all the added sugar and big effort. It's rich, and you feel like you made some-thing, but you didn't really do much. Alternatively, you can warm it up with whole milk and cinnamon.*

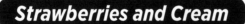

### Strawberries and Cream

**PREP TIME: 10 MINUTES**

*Whip 2 cups organic heavy cream with ¼ cup powdered sugar and 1 tbsp. vanilla until solid peaks form. Spoon over fresh strawberries in a bowl. Store cream in an airtight con-tainer in the fridge.*

## Basic Cobbler

**PREP TIME: 40 MINUTES**

There are lots of options here for fruits, toppings, spices, even size of pan. Use whatever is in season and whatever is available.

*Lightly cook 4 cups fruit (pears, apples, berries, peaches) in 3 tbsp. butter until slightly soft. Mix in about ¼ cup sugar (more or less depending on sweetness of fruit), 1 tsp. vanilla, lemon zest, and juice of ½ lemon, plus cinnamon/clove/nutmeg, if desired. Place in bottom of buttered baking pan (about 8" x 10" if you like it more crispy, smaller if you want it more like a pie). For the topping, there are a few options. 1) Crush almond, amaretto, or ginger cookies, combine with flour, a pinch of salt and butter, and then spread on top. 2) Blend ½ cup butter (1 stick), 1 cup gluten-free flour, 1 cup oatmeal, and a pinch of salt for the topping. 3) Mix 3 tbsp. melted butter, ¼ cup brown sugar, ½ cup spelt flour, 1 tsp. baking powder, pinch of salt, ½ cup oats, and 1 cup milk, and pour over fruit. Bake at 350 degrees for about 30 minutes.*

## Oatmeal-Chocolate-Chip Cookies

**COOK TIME: 40 MINUTES**

This is my go-to when I want to make a treat but don't want to feel too guilty about it.

*In one bowl, sift 1 cup gluten-free flour, ¾ cup white wheat or spelt flour, 1 tsp. baking soda, and ½ tsp. salt. Set aside. In another bowl, mix 1 cup organic butter (softened), ½ cup brown sugar, ½ cup white sugar, ¼ cup almond milk, 1 tsp. vanilla, and 2 large eggs. Gently fold the flour mixture into the butter mixture. Then add 2 cups oats, 1 cup chocolate chips, and 1 cup chopped pecans or walnuts. Drop by teaspoonful on cookie sheet, and bake 10 minutes at 350 degrees. Cool on wire rack to crispen. If you have any left over, store in airtight container.*

## Flan

PREP TIME: 20 MINUTES

I wrote this recipe down from memory after witnessing a young woman make it under the withering eyes of her famous-chef mother-in-law. I figured if she could do it under those conditions, I ought to be able to do it in the safety of my own home. I think I must have remembered correctly, because it works every time.

*Put in blender for a minute or two: 1 can condensed milk, 2 "cans" whole milk, 3 eggs, 1 tsp. corn starch. Burn ¾ cup sugar in a Bundt pan (hold over your stove until sugar is brown and liquid). Pour contents of blender into Bundt pan, place in a larger pan with 2" water in it, and bake at 375 degrees for 1 hour. Cool completely, and then turn out onto a flat plate. Refrigerate 1 day for best results.*

CHAPTER XII

# EATING ON THE GO

*How to keep the faith on the road*

# REBECCA'S TAKE

We all find ourselves on the move. Be it business travel, family visits, or chaperoning our kids to tournaments, classes, and competitions, there are all too many moments without a kitchen and our go-to tools for making healthy food choices. So what do you do to be healthy and economical when you are living out of a car or a hotel room with your kids?

For me, it's always been about planning ahead. If I'm driving, I pack coolers full of water and high-protein, nutrient-rich foods that do not need to be cooked or can be microwaved. I make pasta or grain-based salads in advance. Driving or flying, I scope out the grocery options wherever I'm headed, and, if I'm staying in a hotel, I always call and ask for a fridge and/or a microwave. I've made quesadillas, grain bowls, granola, and yogurt bowls, eggs, oatmeal, and many other staples for my dancer daughter and avoided room service and fast food very often. Nobody's perfect, and I don't try to be. I just try not to go crazy and feel disgusting. Generally, that's achievable.

Here's a list of what I bring or buy upon arrival: cereal, yogurt, dried cranberries, dried *goji* berries, granola, whole-wheat tortillas, peanut or almond butter, jam, micro-waveable oatmeal, rice and pasta, wholesome protein or snack bars, apples, oranges, grapes, chocolate chips, sliced organic cheese, bagged, triple-washed salad greens.

# SHELLEY'S TAKE

Eating on the go with kids brings back some intense memories for me. I am perfectly happy with a peanut-butter-and-jelly sandwich and an apple, and my kids' go-to was certainly a turkey and alfalfa-sprout sandwich with mayo. But kids can be picky, and when you have a very lean child whose performance on the soccer pitch is directly related to his fuel consumption, a mom can get a little crazy.

So, during my eldest son's first few years of soccer games and tournaments, I remember spending Thursday night cooking: I made tins of healthy muffins, homemade energy bars, and Rice Krispie treats so he would have healthy snacks before, during, and after games.

**Energy Bars**

PREP TIME: 30 MINUTES

COOKING TIME: 25 MINUTES

*Warm 1 cup of orange juice, add 1 cup dried, chopped apricots, cover, and let stand. As with all baking, assemble dry ingredients separately: Mix together 1 cup spelt or gluten-free flour, ½ cup almond flour, ½ tsp. salt, 2 tbsp. ground seeds, 2 tbsp. wheat germ, 2 tbsp. chopped walnuts, 1 tsp. cinnamon. Add ½ cup honey and ½ cup canola or flax oil to apricot mixture. Stir thoroughly and add to dry ingredients. Press into baking dish, and bake in 350-degree oven for 25 minutes.*

I have to admit that I completely gave up on packing food somewhere between the second and third child. Maybe I just overdid it early on. Maybe the soccer schedules were insane. Maybe I over-reproduced. Maybe it was all three factors and more—but, eventually, it became overwhelming enough just to get out the door, much less with food for four for the weekend. So I resorted to eating at healthier fast-food establishments—with air-conditioning—such as sub shops or Panera-style cafés.

What I did persevere on was drinks—a huge factor in playing outdoor soccer in usually 80-100 degree weather—and always insisted on packing coolers full of proper rehydration drinks. I even went so far one summer as to make my own electrolyte-replacement drinks, in two types, but the kids completely snubbed their noses at them. Adam and I dutifully finished the pitchers. My typical cooler would always have our well water in Nalgenes and also include some mix of the following: sparkling water, coconut water, chocolate milk, San Pellegrino Limonatas, Gatorade, Body Armor, Vitamin Water, Ito En teas.

# CHAPTER XIII

# JUST PLAIN DELICIOUS

*Do you really need a reason?*

Because when all is said and done, food is meant to be eaten and enjoyed.

### Fish "Milanesa"
COOK TIME: 30 MINUTES

(Adapted from the Argentine-beef version)

*Dry fish fillets, and then coat in any combination of breadcrumbs/corn meal/flour, and parsley and salt. Fry in oil, flipping once, until fork reveals inside is cooked through. Or, place on baking platter, squeeze some lemon juice, dab butter, and bake. Thin fillets will take about 3 minutes per side.*

### Master Quiche Recipe
PREP TIME: 20 MINUTES

From this basic foundation, let your creativity go wherever it takes you.

*Preheat oven to 350 degrees. Lay a pie crust in the bottom of a pie pan. Layer grated cheese (I usually use gruyere or parmesan) in the bottom. Next, put sautéed vegetables of your choice with salt, celery seed, and thyme. Good combinations are asparagus and purple onion, cauliflower and shallots, or spinach and garlic. Pour 6-8 eggs mixed up with some cream or half-and-half on top. Bake about 45 minutes. Easy to make ahead of time and in multiples.*

### Pecan Pie
PREP TIME: 15 MINUTES

Originally in my grandmother's handwriting but adapted to a *slightly* less-sweet version. Amazing with fresh-picked pecans.

*Lay a pie crust in pie pan; cover with 2 cups pecans. After melting ¾ stick butter, whisk in 1 cup brown sugar, ¾ cup corn syrup, 2 tbsp. vanilla extract, and 3 beaten eggs, and pour mixture over pecans. Bake at 350 degrees for 50-60 minutes.*

## Guacamole

**PREP TIME: 15 MINUTES**

My most-requested dish on potluck day with friends. I must admit—with good tortilla chips, and margaritas, it's about all I need some nights!

*You can make the pico de gallo ahead of time: Chop and mix 1 onion, 2-4 cloves garlic, juice of ½-1 lime, ½-1 tbsp. salt, plus cilantro and/or jalapeño, according to taste. This mixture stores well in the fridge. At the last minute, add 3 mashed avocados. Stir and put within easy reach.*

## Zopf Bread

**PREP TIME: 30 MINUTES**

Originally made for an elementary school World Fair day (my son's country was Switzerland); our first version off the Internet was unpalatable. Round 2, we experimented and got this one.

*Dissolve 1 tbsp. yeast in 1⅓ cups warm milk. Add 1 egg yolk, 2 tbsp. melted butter, 2 cups white flour, and 1 tbsp. sea salt. Stir. Add 1½ cups more flour, ½ cup at a time. Turn out onto floured surface and knead for 5 minutes. Return to bowl, place in warm spot, cover, and let rise (about 2 hours). Punch down, divide into 3, and roll each part into cylinders. Braid, stretching dough from both ends. Pinch ends together, place on greased cookie sheet, and let rise another 15 minutes. Preheat oven to 425 degrees. Brush loaf with wash of egg white and 1 tbsp. water. Bake 25 minutes.*

## Chilaquiles

COOK TIME: 15 MINUTES

Ate our first at the Pine Cone Diner in northern California; replicated at home from memory, perhaps not quite as delicious but maybe a little healthier.

*Fry 2 corn tortillas (cut into pieces) in 2 tbsp. oil for a few minutes (until they start smelling like chips!). Add 2 eggs—break the yolks; cook another minute until eggs are set in the tortillas, and then flip. Put a big handful of spinach and a sprinkle of Mexican cheese on top. Then break up the pieces and stir, and cook until cheese is melted and greens are wilted. Serve with favorite hot sauce, salsa, chili powder, and/or cayenne pepper. Can top with avocado slices for a more complete meal.*

## Split Pea Soup

PREP TIME: 20 MINUTES

My ultimate winter comfort food; with fresh bread, a perfect meal!

*Saute 1 onion, 4 cloves garlic, 4 stalks celery, 1 potato, and 4 carrots in olive oil, salt, celery seed, and thyme in large soup pot. Add 1 cup split peas and ½ cup barley. After toasted, add boiling water (about 2 L). Bring to a boil, and then simmer 1 hour. Turn off and cover. Best made in advance and reheated.*

## Grilled Tuna, Avocado, Cucumber, Sesame Seeds, and Sushi Rice

PREP TIME: 25 MINUTES

We used to go out for sushi/Japanese with the kids to try to get them eating other flavors that I couldn't cook myself. It was so expensive, but I thought I could never replicate those flavors. Then I discovered *ponzu* and *mirin*, along with sesame oil and sesame seeds.

*Brush tuna with sesame oil, and marinate in 2 tbsp. of ponzu and 2 tbsp. of mirin. Grill on a panini maker or outdoor grill. Cube 2 avocados and 2 cucumbers, and marinate in the same mixture, 1 tsp. of sesame oil, 2 tbsp. of ponzu and mirin. Add about ¼ cup of white sesame seeds and ¼ cup of black sesame seeds. Slice or cube the fish; mix it in with the avocado and cucumbers. Serve over sushi rice.*

**Variations:** *Vegan with tofu, other grilled fish if you can't find tuna.*

And speaking of grilling here are a few easy classics. Outdoor cooking, whether over a BBQ or an open fire, is so fun and primal.

### Grilled Portabella Mushrooms
PREP TIME: 10 MINUTES

*Simply slice, brush on some canola oil, balsamic vinegar, and sprinkle some salt. Grill until soft. You can also do other vegetables such as zucchini or ½ Romaine lettuce head.*

### Shrimp Kebobs
PREP TIME: 10 MINUTES

*Marinate in lime juice, canola oil, salt, and your favorite hot sauce for a few hours. Skewer and grill, flipping once, until they turn pink.*

### Festive Salad
PREP TIME: 30 MINUTES

I started making this with my kids for holiday meals. They thought it was a fun way to eat salad. Then, as they got older, they started bringing it to gatherings with friends—they realized they weren't the only ones who loved it. It's become our own family holiday tradition. It takes a lot of chopping, but that's what makes it special.

*Ingredients: dried cranberries, slivered almonds, Granny Smith apples, iceberg lettuce, chunks of Gruyere (or tofu, or skip it), tons and tons of lemon juice. Chop up the lettuce and Gruyere (into cubes). Add the cranberries. Toast the almonds in the oven with some sea salt (350 degrees, about 15 minutes, but watch them). Make the dressing in a measuring cup—half olive oil, half lemon juice (3-4 lemons), salt and pepper to taste. Don't dress the salad until shortly before you eat it, to keep it fresh and crunchy.*

# CHAPTER XIV

# COOKING LIKE IT MATTERS

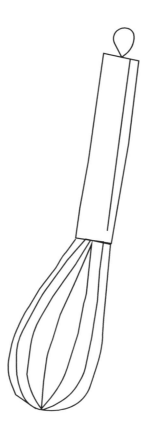

*Be yourself in the kitchen*

Can you talk about anything these days without talking about "mindfulness?" It's every-where. Though it seems absurd, it's become the currency of competition—with all its promised benefits touching everything from career, parenting, weight management, focus, happiness, and physical health, everyone's on the mindfulness train or feeling slightly guilty or compromised if they aren't. And, of course, there's an app for that. Many apps, in fact. It is all too easy to rely on the very technology that is partially responsible for sending anxious, exhausted people on quests for internal, meaningful journeys to mediate those very experiences.

What's available on our phones, computers, in bookstores, and yoga studios are, in essence, "recipes" with instructions for how to meditate, declutter, tune-in, observe one's thoughts, and maintain presence in the moment. Many of them appear effective for some critical mass of people, though quite a few of them require the commitment of more time or money than the average person possesses.

When I was in high school, I picked up a copy of *Zen and the Art of Motorcycle Maintenance*. Though I'd read some good books at that point it my life, it was one of the first times that I began to see the layers in literature. Not because I was particularly enlightened, but because the book was quite demonstrative in its attempt to attach lofty and philosophical meaning to ordinary things, people, and activities. It wasn't really about Buddhism or motorcycles—at least not in a way that my sixteen-year-old self could tease out—it was about the personal exercise of assigning meaning. When I think of my own time in the kitchen, I carry forward my teenage experience of reading that book. I assign meaning to what I'm doing: it isn't just practical—it's metaphysical.

When you contemplate the activity of preparing food to nourish yourself, the exten-sion to bigger issues is natural. The act of your hands peeling a carrot, slicing some bread, or whisking up a concoction connects you to those who did those things for you when you were too small to do them yourself. When you do them for your children, you feel that you are continuing the chain started by your great grandparents. When you practice these habits and teach them, by example, to your kids, there's something deeply emotional and profoundly intellectual going on. If you allow yourself the space to observe this, you can see that your mind is a creative engine. It allows you to contem-plate your place in the cosmos and to define yourself simply by repeating the actions required to prepare a meal.

What's more, there's a freedom that comes from confidence. Once you know what you can do, what you have always done, and what your grandmother did, you can begin to improvise. You know the foundation and can begin to innovate and progress by simply considering "What if?" So, throw in those dried cranberries, add more spinach for color, or try a substitution that aligns with your values, resources, or whims.

Put it all together. Make it work. Cook like it matters.

# ACKNOWLEDGMENTS

The authors gratefully thank their children, Dylan, Nathan, Aidan, Samantha, and Olivia; their husbands, Adam and Jeff; and their siblings, parents, and grandparents. Our families are the joy of our lives and the central focus of our food journeys. They are also remarkable readers and generous critics. Additionally, we thank special friends who encouraged us. Readers, reactors, and listeners extraordinaire Alex Ota, Julia Nicholls, Olivia Nicholls, Kristina Austin Nicholls, Cristina Vitale, Kim Sommer, Lisa Otsuka, Yvonne Tally, and Jack Coolbaugh. Last, each thanks the other for a magical and seamless experience as well as over thirty years of friendship and respect.

# RECIPE INDEX

Made in the USA
San Bernardino, CA
15 January 2019